ROADSIDE SURVIVAL

LOW-TECH SOLUTIONS TO AUTOMOBILE BREAKDOWNS

WALT BRINKER

ISBN: 978-1-63068-589-8
Library of Congress Control Number: 2014901696
Lightning Source Publishing Platform

Table of Contents

Acknowledgements vii

Foreword ix

Walt's Top 10 Roadside Survival Tips xv

Chapter 1
Big Picture 1
 Telephone Numbers (by State) for
 Non-emergencies/Roadside Assistance 2

Chapter 2
Safety 5
 Safely Positioning Your Vehicle 5
 Use of Reflecting Devices 6
 Unwanted "Help" 10

Chapter 3
Tire-related Issues 13
 Buying Tires 13
 List of Tire-related Issues 15
 Solutions to Common Tire-related Issues 22

Tire Care   23
Air Pressure   23
Temporary Repair of a Flat Tire   26
Changing a Flat Tire   27
Protection from Getting Dirty or Wet   27
Hand Protection   29
Solutions to Spare Tire Issues   30
Spare Tire On Board?   30
Can the Spare Tire be Made Available for Use?   32
Is the Spare Tire Rim the Correct One for
the Vehicle?   34
Is the Spare Tire Fully Inflated?   36
Is the Spare Tire in Good Condition, Safe for Use?   37
How Old is the Spare Tire?   37
Solutions to Typical Problems Removing and Mounting Tires   38
Capability to Loosen Lug Nuts/Bolts   38
Aftermarket Rims: Lug Wrench May Not Work   41
Rounded Lug Nuts   42
Wheel Locks (also known as "Locking Lug Nuts")   43
Requirement for Deep Socket   44
Extension Bar for "Standoff" Situations   44
Removal (and Replacement) of Loosened Lug Nuts   45
Removal of Rim Stuck to Vehicle Wheel   47
Solutions to Typical Problems with Vehicle Jacks   49
Proper Jack and Lift Points for Your Vehicle   49
Jack Stability   50
Jacks for Trailers   54
Maneuvering Tires   55
Spacers   56
Changing a Tire at Night   56

Chapter 4
"Out of Gas" Issues   61
Running Out of Gas   61

"Rock the Car" 61
Regular vs. Premium Gas 62
What are the Reasons Folks Run Out of Gas? 63

Chapter 5
Engine Overheating Issues 67
Causes of Overheating 67
Warning Signs 67
Preventing Overheating Breakdowns 67
Dealing With Overheating Breakdowns 69

Chapter 6
Engine Cuts Off and Will Not Re-start 71
Loose Battery Cables 71
Battery Connection Cleaning 73
The "Paperclip Trick" 73
Jumper Cables 76
Correct Sequence When Using Jumper Cables 76
Dead Battery/Bad Alternator Charging Problems 78
Bad Alternator – Not Always a Show Stopper 79
Thin Jumper Cables vs. Thick jumper Cables 80
Push Start 81
Fuel Pump Cutoff Switches in Ford Motor
Company Vehicles 82

Chapter 7
Motorist is Locked out of Vehicle 85
Dealing with Lock Outs 86

Chapter 8
Suggested Items to Contend with Vehicle Breakdowns 89
"Suggested" Items Not Already Stowed with Vehicle 90
Stowage of Items on "Suggested" List 94
Additional Items Walt Carries "On Patrol" 95

Chapter 9
Win-Win Hobby   97

Walt's Top 10 Reasons for Making Roadside Assists   101

Glossary of Terms   103

About the Author   107

Acknowledgements

I had plenty of help writing this book. I already knew most of the technical information (the "meat"), but I needed advice and assistance with packaging. Aware that most other folks do not share my level of interest in the details of roadside survival, I needed to add "taste" to the meat and tidy up the text to make it palatable to the average reader.

My special thanks to the following for their considerable constructive, patient help with formatting, flow, clarity and wording during development of the manuscript: Ken Carlson; Joel Gartenberg; Ron Meier; Sam Champi; Ed Johnson; Jim Muldoon; Steve Stephens; Joe FitzHarris; Rex Nichols; Robert Vowell; Paul Mlakar; Jim Dickens; Paul Roggenkamp; Mike McKay; Al Cito; Peyton Ligon; Ginger Holland; John Weaver, who advised me on publishers and marketing; Vardell Nesmith; Mikel Gore; Bill Petruzel; my wife, Betsy; and my sisters, Marie Koenig and Ann Schwall.

Katy Brinker, my lovely daughter, demonstrates in Chapter 3 the ease of using various tools to change tires.

Myra Linder Bell, a cousin and family friend, also a professional book designer, prepared diagrams showing correct deployment of reflecting warning triangles. She also contributed common sense ideas including the book's title, and lots of informed encouragement.

Brian Ashbaugh, an attorney friend, provided helpful legal advice during my discussions with various publishers.

For granting me permissions to use photographs from their past articles about my "Win-Win Hobby": Mike Adams, Executive Editor of "The Fayetteville Observer" newspaper in Fayetteville, North Carolina; and Lisa Fredrickson, Executive Publisher of "Absolutely Katy", a community magazine in Katy, Texas.

Last, and certainly not least, I thank my daughter-in-law Toni and three of her kids (my grandchildren), Ben, Lily and Lucy, for posing for the picture on the cover. Their sister, Andi, was too busy riding her bicycle to participate.

Foreword

The primary purpose for this book is to empower motor vehicle drivers to prevent and contend with breakdowns so as not to become stranded.

Imagine your son (or daughter) driving back home alone across the state. The time is 6:30 PM, it's beginning to get dark, and home is two hours away. Suddenly he hears a loud "whoosh" on the right side of the car; at the same time, the car begins to vibrate and pulls to the right, and the steering seems unresponsive. Fortunately, he guides the car onto the highway shoulder where it comes to a stop. He gets out, sees that the right front tire has blown out and has been shredded, and he calls you from a cell phone and describes what happened. He has never before changed a tire and cannot find the spare tire or any tire changing tools. Could this happen to someone you love?

Two hundred million licensed motor vehicle drivers in the United States expose themselves routinely to significant risk while betting that they will not become stranded when they drive. There are two kinds of drivers: 1) those who have already experienced a disabled vehicle (and will again), and 2) those who will for the first time. National Highway Traffic Safety Administration (NHTSA) estimates that 5.8 million vehicle crashes of all types occur annually in the US (average for 2005-2015). This compares with 30 million yearly calls for assistance to AAA alone (33 million in 2017); I know from experience that this number from AAA represents only a small fraction of total breakdowns. So, breakdowns are at very least five times as likely as crashes; I believe that this figure is much higher. I estimate that the ratio of breakdowns to crashes is around 20:1. So, it's not a matter of whether you will break down; it's a matter of when, where, and how often.

Drivers can decrease the chances that they will have a breakdown and become stranded. This subject may seem dry and boring until you have experienced being stranded and vulnerable to whims of anyone who comes along. Some folks learn only by experiencing inconvenience, embarrassment, and potentially serious risks. Others make the proactive choice to learn how to prevent problems and the methods to counteract them should they occur. The safest breakdown is the one prevented and never happens; the safest breakdown that happens is the one with least risk (which normally is a function of time stranded). This book provides you with the opportunity to avoid the negatives associated with becoming stranded (including no bathroom, no water, no food, too cold, too hot, insects, darkness, and encountering predators – human and others).

Some folks ask, "Why should I worry about breakdowns? I'll just call for XYZ commercial roadside assistance." I don't knock these assist companies. I can confirm that they usually provide good service in places where they use their own people and equipment, although they're not always timely. Problems occur with breakdowns away from their offices where they often subcontract the work to third stringers who are incompetent. I have seen a lot of this. But why not focus on preventing breakdowns in the first place?

The first time I recall helping another motorist was in 1980 when I encountered a lady in a car whose engine had stopped. I used my jumper cables to jump start her engine. It was Christmas season, and I remember how good I felt bringing such relief to that lady. So, I began to look for vehicles "in distress". Occasionally, then, I would stop for others, but there was little I could do unless all they needed was a simple jump start. So, I began acquiring knowledge, tools and equipment which enabled me to perform other simple assists, like changing flat tires, fixing battery connections, opening locked doors, and adding water to cooling systems and fuel to empty gas tanks. The more times I tried, the more I realized what knowledge and tools I lacked. Over time, learning new techniques and acquiring new tools has helped me rise to a much higher level and convinced me that I should share my knowledge with others who could benefit.

I have made well over 2,000 roadside assists free-of-charge as a hobby. No two have been alike; however, definitive trends and patterns have emerged. I have structured this book to focus on the major causes for breaking down and becoming stranded. A motorist can break down and not be stranded provided he (or she) is able to bail himself out.

My observations and advice are the product of performing those roadside assists, not all of which went like clockwork. Much of what I learned came from trial and error, adjusting to situations where I initially lacked either knowledge or tools to get the job done. Other knowledge came from research on the internet and talking with experts like Robert Ramlal, my friend and super-mechanic in Houston, Texas. My format mixes accounts of actual assists with discussion of why the help was necessary, and what the drivers could have done to prevent becoming stranded in the first place.

I am not a mechanic, and most vehicle breakdowns do not require a mechanic. My solutions are simple, low tech, easily understood, and enable a driver of a disabled vehicle to drive it off an interstate highway or parking lot, to a facility which can fix the problem, or so that the motorist can obtain items needed to prevent recurrence. They are not meant to be permanent repairs.

Most breakdowns occur for reasons I can fix (and teach you to prevent and fix); however I cannot fix serious mechanical issues. About all I can do in such cases is to ensure that the motorist knows where he is, provide the name, address and phone number of a repair shop, let him use my cell phone to call for help, and give him a bottle of drinking water.

Common sense says that tending to routine maintenance of all the vehicle's systems, including lubrication (especially the engine's oil, its lifeblood), cooling, electrical, ignition, brakes, and tires, goes a long way to ensure long, safe vehicle life and good reliability – resulting in fewer breakdowns.

If you know someone (wife, husband, daughter, son, friend, even yourself) who drives and would benefit from being able to 1) prevent breaking down, and 2) rescue himself from situations most likely to otherwise render him stranded, this book is what the doctor ordered. Generally, good luck comes to those who help themselves; this book is for those in that group. If you would like to change the mind of someone currently not in that group, send him a copy of this book and insist he read it. Some drivers live in denial that they could break down; this book can help them see otherwise and show them how to prevent, prepare for and contend with that eventuality.

The key to getting maximum benefit from this book is not to just stick it in your car's glove compartment and plan to whip it out and save yourself when you break down! You should read it ahead of time to help prevent breaking down; then pick up my suggested tools and other gear to enable you to help yourself should it happen.

Some of my assist recipients had been waiting a long time for commercial roadside assistance. A few wanted to keep waiting, but most agreed to let me assist. Several, after watching me work (or, as I do often, coach the driver as he uses his own tools, or mine, as necessary), told me that next time they'll be able to bail themselves out without assistance. More than a few have told me that their commercial assisters sent incompetent subcontracted help who couldn't fix the problem.

Out on the road I have met many characters who added levity:

- On the way home from work I pulled over for a car with a flat tire. The driver was a nice-looking 40-something year old woman (I was 64). The tire change was routine and quick, and when I finished, she thanked me and then looked me in the eye and asked earnestly, **"Are you married?"** Surprised, I responded that yes, I was. Betsy, my wife, got a chuckle when I told her about it.

- On another highway assist for a car with a flat tire, the occupants were a woman driver and her teenage daughter. This tire change also was routine and quick. When I finished, the daughter, noting my "Purple Heart" license plate, asked me, **"Does that license plate mean that you have to do this?"** I told her, no, that I just did it because I like to.

- After a similar tire change assist, the driver, a man even older than I, asked me directly, **"Are you a minister?"** I had to confess that I was not.

I hope this book also inspires readers to help others; check out the "Win-Win Hobby" chapter. Along the way, helpers help themselves. I can make any good day better by performing a roadside assist. For me, the rush begins when I first see a disabled vehicle, and the feeling lasts for hours after I am done. I realize that my hobby is not for everyone: "Different strokes for different folks". Still, even without all the gear I carry, almost anyone with some equipment and basic knowledge from this book can make a difference. Why not you? I'm not suggesting that you should do something you wouldn't do otherwise. There are risks involved, and you need to weigh risk versus benefit.

For additional information about roadside survival, visit my website: http://www.roadsidesurvival.com/

Walt's Top 10
Roadside Survival Tips

The real "meat" supporting these tips is in the chapters which follow: An ounce of prevention is worth a pound of cure!

1. Prevent tire failures by having tires inspected and balanced by tire professionals every 5,000 miles. Replace worn out tires. Fix poor wheel alignment, which can cause premature tire wear and failure.

2. Prevent tire failures by frequent checks of tire air pressures, especially before long trips, <u>using a tire pressure gauge</u> (the only accurate method); then ensure correct pressure.

3. Do not drive around without a serviceable spare tire (maximum six years old), designed for your vehicle (spare tire rims are designed for specific vehicles) – fully inflated, or with means to inflate, like a 12-volt air compressor.

4. Do not drive around without jack and tire changing tools which actually work on your vehicle and its wheels (you need to verify that they all fit and work).

5. Practice, using the vehicle's operator manual <u>before</u> the flat tire occurs, removing the spare tire from stowage and mounting it on a vehicle wheel using the vehicle's jack and tire changing tools. Check: Lug nuts too tight? Jack functions OK? Know correct vehicle lift points? Have key to locking wheel lug nuts? Have key to security lock for spare tire?

6. If towing a trailer, pay special attention: Tire age not over six years; have trailer jack, lumber for jack base support, and proper size wrench for lug nuts; have at least one spare tire (not older than six years) with means to inflate if needed; ensure spare tire can be removed from trailer for use (sticking due to rust is a common problem).

7. Check tightness of battery connections monthly (they should not be moveable by hand); tighten if needed, and keep the correct wrench handy with the vehicle.

8. Have 20-feet long jumper cables in the vehicle; know how to use them to jump start an engine and charge a dead battery.

9. Have a cell phone and its 12-volt battery charger in the vehicle. Then, if you need help, you can call for it. Have a road atlas, in case you are far from home with a broken GPS, so you can describe your location accurately.

10. Listen/pay attention to your vehicle; it will "tell" you when it is about to fail: Wheel vibration/pulling to the side/mushy handling/low tire pressure light indicate a tire with low air pressure; weak engine starts and dim lights indicate loose battery clamps or failing battery; engine temperature gauge reads hot; battery light on means the battery is not being charged and will soon fail, causing the engine to stop; other warning lights; unusual noises from brakes, wheels, transmission or engine; funny odors; excess or white exhaust; fluid leaks. Then, fix problems before they become failures.

Chapter 1

Big Picture

By far the most common reasons for becoming stranded are tire-related: 75% of my assists. Discussion of tire-related reasons follows the chapter on safety.

The remaining 25% are split roughly equally among the following reasons, which will be covered in separate chapters:

- Out of gas

- Engine overheating

- Engine cuts off and will not re-start due to loose battery connection or battery is dead or too weak

- Motorist is locked out of vehicle

First priority should be to <u>prevent</u> breaking down through smart planning, awareness and preparation; however, sometimes events beyond one's control intervene and cause a breakdown anyway. At that point the focus shifts to contending with the situation and getting back on the road safely.

Telephone Numbers (by State)
for Non-emergencies/Roadside Assistance

Often I meet stranded motorists who have summoned help from commercial agencies or friends, but the help is overdue by hours. Many states have a non-emergency telephone number to contact the highway patrol, which will dispatch an officer who may try to solve the immediate problem; this officer also can call for a tow truck, but the tow likely will be not free. These numbers, particularly handy when driving in states other than your own, may be used also to report road hazards, such as a tire retread on the highway.

State	Non-emergency Telephone Number
AL, MS, NC, SC	*47
AR	1-501-618-8100
CO	*277
CT, DE, MA, WA, VT	911
FL	*347
GA, ID	*477
IA	1-800-525-5555
IL	*999
IN	1-317-232-8248; Then 7
KS	*47; *582 (turnpike only)
KY	1-800-222-5555
LA	*577
ME	1-207-626-3800
MD, NJ, VA	#77
MO, NE, OK	*55
MT	1-855-647-3777
NH, RI, WV	*77
NM	1-505-827-9301
NV	*647
OH	#677
PA	411
TN	*847

TX	*377
UT	1-801- 887-3800
WY	1-307-777-4321

Phone Numbers (by State) for Non-emergencies/Roadside Assistance. Phone numbers for the table were acquired from various state law enforcement agency websites and other online government sources. States not shown apparently do not use a single number; several states instead use local numbers.

Some cities have special government-sponsored roadside assistance teams available with a phone call; however, their coverage is not widespread. If one is lucky a state highway patrolman or a Good Samaritan will just appear, but several of my assist recipients have told me they waited for hours before someone (like you or me) stopped. This leaves self-help as an option which never should be dismissed.

Chapter 2

Safety

If I didn't feel safe performing roadside assists, I would not do them; and I certainly would not suggest that you get out of your vehicle on an Interstate highway shoulder to change a flat tire or do anything else. I have passed up many, many opportunities to perform assists because I judged the situations unsafe for me. When a disabled vehicle is not in a location with room to work safely, when traffic seems too fast or reckless for conditions, or when I cannot stop safely, especially at night or in rain, I keep driving and do not stop.

Safely Positioning Your Vehicle

I have the option to keep moving when I see a broken down vehicle. So do you. But the driver of a vehicle which has become disabled does not always have that choice. The driver of a vehicle with flat tire often can keep moving his vehicle on the flat tire rim to a location where he will be relatively safe, either to wait for help or try to bail himself out. On many highways there is no shoulder on which to park, so here the only good choice with a flat tire, especially in heavy traffic, is to turn on the car's hazard warning flashers and keep driving slowly on the rim until one can get out of traffic to a shoulder, exit, rest area, gas station, or parking lot. This most likely will destroy your tire, and it may damage the rim, but your safety trumps a rim and a tire. If the vehicle's disability causes its engine to quit, driver choices are more limited. Hopefully the driver can steer the vehicle to a safe place, such as a highway shoulder, before it stops rolling. If there is no such safe haven, driver options depend on factors such as traffic density and speed, and whether he can summon a tow truck to pull the vehicle to safety or a repair shop. If the breakdown occurs on a divided highway, such as an Interstate, ending up on the right shoulder is almost always better than stopping on the left median – which usually has less hard-surface space and is closer to faster oncoming traffic in the passing lane. Instead of assisting drivers in the median I usually have them carefully reposition their vehicles to the right shoulder, even if it means driving a short distance on a flat tire. If traffic is heavy and fast and the vehicle is blocking a lane of traffic the stranded driver likely is better off getting out of his vehicle in case it should get hit by another, an all too common occurrence.

My "line" when first meeting a stranded motorist is, "What do you need?" Here, I have just stopped for a vehicle on the shoulder of Interstate 95 in North Carolina, and I am walking back to meet its driver. Photo was taken by a Fayetteville Observer photographer during a "patrol" with staff writer Chick Jacobs, who wrote a story about my hobby. My headlights and fog lights are always on in daytime as a safety measure so others can see me better. Use of this photo is with permission of executive editor of "Fayetteville Observer" newspaper.

Use of Reflecting Devices

When I stop to assist a vehicle along the highway, my main concern is my safety, primarily from oncoming traffic which typically passes within yards of the disabled vehicle. So, my first actions after determining the driver's problem and deciding to stay and assist, especially when traffic is heavy or during poor visibility, are to ensure the vehicle's hazard warning flashers are turned on, don my bright orange reflective vest, and then deploy my three reflecting warning triangles. Correct triangle placement (assuming the vehicle is in a right lane or on a right shoulder) is as follows. On a 1-way highway, or shoulder: Behind the disabled vehicle's left rear corner within 10 feet, and behind the vehicle 100 feet and 200 feet in the center of the vehicle's lane or shoulder. On a 2-way highway, or its shoulder: Behind the disabled vehicle's left rear corner within 10 feet, and behind the vehicle 100 feet in the center of the vehicle's lane or shoulder; also, 100 feet in front of the vehicle in the center of the vehicle's lane or its shoulder. Positioning the close-in and farther triangles like this: 1) accentuates the warning and direction to stay clear, and 2) reduces chances that the farther triangles will be blown over unnoticed. If the vehicle location is just over a hill, or around a sharp turn that obstructs line-of-sight vision, move the farthest triangle(s) to the other side of the hill or curve.

ONE-WAY OR DIVIDED HIGHWAY

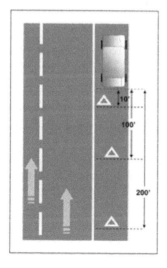

TWO-WAY OR UNDIVIDED HIGHWAY

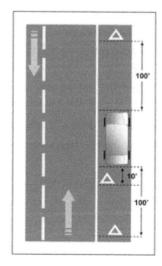

OBSTRUCTED VIEW – CURVE

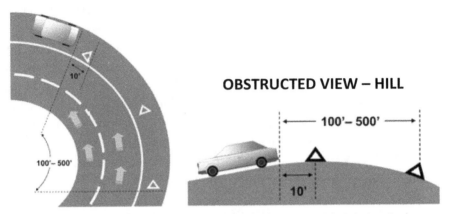

OBSTRUCTED VIEW – HILL

Correct placement of reflecting warning triangles (per written descriptions in the U.S. Department of Transportation's Federal Motor Carrier Safety Administration Rules and Regulations, dated July 16, 2013, Subpart C, Paragraph 392.22). All diagrams show the disabled vehicle on the highway shoulder; same deployment of triangles on a travel lane would apply if the vehicle could not move to a shoulder. "Obstructed View" diagram of a curve depicts a One-Way or Divided Highway; for a Two-Way highway the middle triangle would instead go in front of the vehicle. "Obstructed View" diagram for a hill on a 2-way undivided highway assumes that the third triangle is in front of the car. Illustrations above were created from the DOT regulation's written description by Myra Linder Bell, a professional designer.

Retrieving the triangles is the last thing I do before departing the scene. Recently I acquired two nifty "9-in-1 Safety Puck" red flashing LEDs which are equipped with magnets. Both go on the top rear of the disabled vehicle (which is behind mine) during night stops. During night assists I lend a flashlight to an adult and have him face oncoming traffic from behind the disabled vehicle. His job is to watch the traffic and wave it away from the shoulder toward the highway.

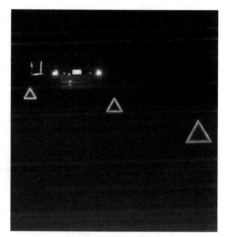

Reflecting warning triangles are the best way to highlight a disabled vehicle. Note the correct placement of triangles, shown here for a 1-way or divided highway.

Reflecting warning triangles, vehicle hazard warning flashers, and reflecting vest (seen here from rear-approaching traffic's perspective) provide extra margin of safety, especially at night or during poor day visibility.

Flares are an alternative to reflecting warning triangles. However, unlike triangles, flares have a storage shelf life and they eventually burn out.

Walt Recommends: As a minimum, keep in each vehicle a set of three warning triangles; deploy them if your vehicle becomes disabled, especially during limited visibility. Also, have a bright colored reflecting vest for wear outside your vehicle.

Unwanted "Help"

Another safety concern is unwanted "help" from others who may have a different agenda.

During an assist of a family from Maryland whose vehicle had a flat tire on an Interstate 95 exit ramp during a trip to Florida, the stranded motorist had walked up the ramp to a service station to use an air pump to reflate his flat spare tire. An intoxicated man at the station had followed the motorist back to his vehicle and was there when I arrived on site. As the motorist and I tried to reflate his spare tire, this man kept interfering, repeatedly announcing that he was "half Sioux and half black", showing me photos of his family, and trying to shake hands with me. I told him several times that the motorist and I had the situation under control, and that we didn't need his help.

Finally, after he would not leave us alone, I told the man directly and very firmly to leave. Luckily he did. In this case, the spare tire had a bad leak and the hour was late, so we had to make several phone calls from my list of tire stores in Fayetteville to find one with the correct tire size, and drive there in my car, with his original rim with flat tire, before the store closed. The assist was a huge success, and the family has thanked me repeatedly.

While your vehicle is broken down, are you safer inside the vehicle, or outside? You are safer from oncoming vehicles if you are outside. Unless you have credible means of self-defense to deter or protect (hardy appearance, martial arts experience, armed), you are somewhat safer from unwanted "help" if you are inside; however, a determined unwanted "helper" can easily break your window. So, my view is that the sooner you get moving again, the safer you will be. This generally means exercising the "self-help" option to become un-stranded. This is one of the many reasons why I wrote this book.

Chapter Summary:

1. If possible, move the disabled vehicle out of traffic, off the road; if a tire is flat, drive on it anyway to get the vehicle off the road.

2. Deploy warning devices correctly to highlight your location to oncoming traffic.

3. Consider your own safety – in or out of the vehicle.

4. Expedite repairs, even if temporary, using self-help if possible.

Chapter 3

Tire-related Issues

Since tire failures play a disproportionate role in vehicle breakdowns, <u>by far the best preventive measure is ensuring that your vehicle's tires are in good condition.</u>

Buying Tires

I recommend strongly against buying used tires; you will be inheriting someone else's problems, some of which are invisible time bombs. When purchasing new tires, it's wise to also buy optional "free" inspection, rotation and balancing. Then, by bringing the vehicle in every 5,000 miles, the tires are maintained by professionals, ensuring maximum tire life and safety. When buying new tires, it's also smart to buy a plan for "free" replacement if a tire is damaged, which covers replacements from blowouts, damage to a sidewall (which cannot be repaired), and damage from hitting debris on the highway – all of which are major reasons for failures of tires in good condition.

Each time I have purchased a new set of tires something has happened to at least one of them to warrant a replacement. While at the tire dealer ask to have the spare tire checked too. Do yourself and your loved ones a favor: follow the advice above, which will have a huge impact on your safety and whether your vehicle will break down.

With one of my sons on board late one afternoon for a demonstration of roadside assisting, I encountered a man on the shoulder of Interstate 10 with his wife and two dogs in a Chevrolet Suburban with a flat left rear tire. When I asked the driver what he needed, he replied that he would not need my help since he had a commercial roadside assistance policy, and he expected them to show up very soon. He thanked me for stopping. I handed him my card with address and telephone number, and I departed. My son and I went home and had just finished supper when the telephone rang. The fellow with the Suburban was on the line. After identifying himself, he asked very politely whether I would mind coming back to his location. He said that the commercial assistance guy showed up, but he was an idiot and couldn't even find his jack. I told him I would be there soon.

This assist happened just before I had acquired my jack for pickups and large vans and SUVs and the additional pieces of lumber I now use to provide increased elevation and stability for my primary hydraulic jack. I knew that I needed a jack which would fit under the Suburban's axle and provide lots of lift, so I stopped at the home of a neighbor with a Suburban and borrowed his jack – just in case the motorist didn't have one. Back at the site of the disabled Suburban (by now it was evening and dark) I found his tire changing tools (stowed, as expected, inside the left rear quarter panel inside the vehicle) and quickly changed his tire. As I expected, his spare tire was low and required additional air – remedied with my 12-volt air compressor. He thanked me very enthusiastically. Since then we have been friends and remain in contact by email. That Christmas he sent me a smoked ham. Another good thing about that evening is that my son got a taste of helping someone else.

As I said earlier, three quarters of my assist recipients have been stranded due to tire-related issues. Here is a collection, from personal experiences with assists, of reasons motorists become stranded due to tire-related issues (most issues apply to trailers as well).

List of Tire-related Issues

Before gagging on this long list of "issues" and concluding that "self-help" will not be your option, please realize that none of these problems would have occurred in the first place if the motorists had planned and prepared ahead, been aware of potential problems, and used common sense. As you read these issues, ask yourself whether you and your vehicle might be "guilty"; then continue reading to my preventive, common sense "solutions" to these issues:

- Motorist does not want to get dirty or wet by getting on the ground to position a jack, or handle the flat tire and spare tire.

- Motorist has no means to protect hands from touching exposed sharp steel bands resulting from a tire blowout or tread separation.

- Spare tire is not available. Some cars are sold new without a spare tire, relying on "run flat" tires, which are useless if torn up by debris on the highway. More often, the spare tire which came with the vehicle simply is missing.

- Spare tire is on a rim which will not fit on the car's wheel since the rim is not the original or made for that vehicle (spare tire rims are designed only for specific vehicles).

- Spare tire cannot be removed from the vehicle (spare tire rim is secured by a lock whose key cannot be found; or spare rim's wing nut fastener is so corroded that it cannot be unscrewed; or for pickups and some large vans: spare tire lowering mechanism is jammed, cannot find the sectioned shaft tool which activates the lowering mechanism, or the plastic guide tube from the hole in or near the rear bumper to the lowering mechanism is not aligned with the mechanism's contact point).

- Spare tire is flat or significantly underinflated so it will not perform safely when mounted on the vehicle; driver has no means to reflate the tire.

- Spare tire is flat (usually has been flat for a long time) and will not hold air due to lack of a seal between the rubber tire and the metal rim.

- Spare tire is worn out and therefore unsafe and unusable.

- Spare tire is too old to be reliable without blowing out (older than 6 years).

- No lug wrench, or incorrect lug wrench.

All motor vehicles are sold new with correct lug wrench. However, older vehicles may have instead (for a variety of reasons) a different lug wrench which is the wrong size and will not work.

- Lug nuts are too tight for removal with available lug wrench.

- Lug wrench will not work since the walls of the wrench's head are too thick to fit into the opening around the lug nut (this often happens with aftermarket rims, requiring a socket – which has a thinner wall).

Tight gap between lug nut and edge of the hole in this rim will not permit use of lug wrench.

Tight gap between lug nut and inside of its hole in the rim

Compare: thick wall around lug wrench head (left), with thin wall of same-size socket (right). Lug wrench head will not fit in gap between hole and lug nut shown in previous photo; the socket will fit.

- Lug nuts' edged surfaces have become "rounded" from previous improper use of pliers, vise grips, or incorrect size wrench or socket, making their removal impossible without "special tools": "bolt and nut remover" sockets which will bite into the rounded edges.

Lug nut with "rounded" edged surfaces prevents removal from wheel by lug wrench or standard socket.

- Cannot find the key to unlock wheel locks.

- Cannot find security key which attaches to end of the shaft to lower spare tire (Lincoln Aviator SUV, others).

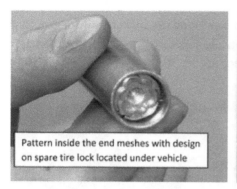

Pattern inside the end meshes with design on spare tire lock located under vehicle

Security key for Lincoln Navigator fits on end of shaft used to lower the spare tire.

- Key lock in rear bumper plug securing access to spare tire is rusted (most often on Chevrolet pickups and Suburbans).

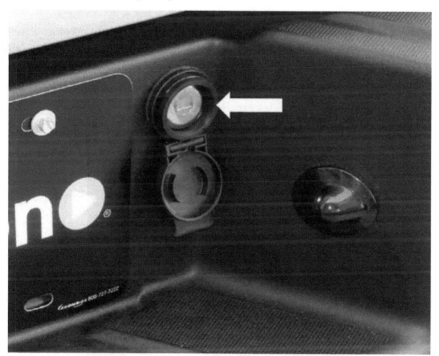

Security lock controlling access to spare tire for many pickups and SUVs is in a plug in rear bumper. Lock opens with ignition key. Lock will become rusty and inoperative unless lubricated. More than once I have had to inject "Liquid Wrench" or "PB Blaster" through a thin plastic straw into rusted locks, and then work the lock with the ignition key to unlock and remove the plug.

- Neither the vehicle's lug wrench nor standard sockets will engage lug nuts because the wheel lugs protrude too far from the wheel through center of the lug nuts; requires deep socket.

Standard socket is not deep enough to fit all the way over lug nut with protruding lug. Result: insufficient grip.

Deep socket is required to accommodate protruding lug and achieve sufficient grip on lug nut.

- Rim to be removed has a "deep dish" shape with lug nuts recessed from the edge of the rim; will require an extension bar from the wrench to the socket which engages the lug nuts (this is common with dual wheel pickups, and some trailers). Most rims will require at least a short extension bar. "Breaker bar" provides excellent leverage to loosen tight nuts.

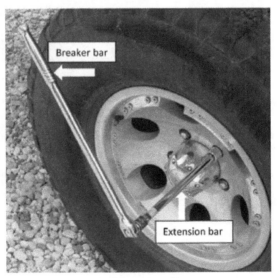

An "extension bar" provides offset in order to access recessed lug nuts.

- Rim with flat tire, after all lug nuts are removed, sticks to the vehicle wheel and cannot be removed by hand.

- No functioning jack, wrong jack, or missing jack components.

- Vehicle, during jack-up, rolls; if this occurs after rim with flat tire is removed, the car's wheel will fall to the ground, often leaving too little clearance to re-insert a jack under the lift point.

- Vehicle jack, under load, sinks into sand, soft soil, or vegetation, preventing lift of vehicle high enough to change the tire; also can cause jack to become unstable, so it cannot lift vertically, and it topples.

- Vehicle jack will not work with trailer, and no suitable jack is available for trailer.

- Spare tire is too heavy to lift and slide on to vehicle wheel lugs; same with some European cars: more difficult because spare tire must be held in position to insert bolts through the rim holes into the receiving holes in the vehicle wheel.

- If spare cannot be used, the flat tire on the original rim must be replaced – a problem unless a tire store with correct tire is open (most close by 5 or 6 PM), and someone else must drive the stranded driver and rim with flat tire to the store, wait for the repair, and then drive back to the immobilized vehicle.

- With some aftermarket rims, a spacer is needed between the rim and the vehicle's wheel to provide slightly more standoff and ensure a correct fit. The spacer fits on the vehicle wheel independent of the rim and remains attached unless removed. If the aftermarket rim with the flat tire is removed and an original equipment rim is used as a spare, the spare will not seat fully on the vehicle wheel unless the spacer is removed.

- Another frequent issue with aftermarket rims is low-profile tires which are easily flattened when the tire hits a speed bump or pothole. Shortage of cushioning and "give" in these tires' sidewall results in their easily being pinched, resulting in a hole in the sidewall and a flat tire. Several folks have complained to me that their low-profile tires also have short tread life.

My most memorable assist of a motorist with a pinched low-profile tire was a fellow in an Audi on Interstate 10. Since his unrepaired spare had also recently been pinched and flattened on a speed bump, we took his rim with flat tire to a Discount Tire store. While there, he told me he owned a store that sold comic books and toy "action figures". He also insisted on paying me for my help. I told him I would take a box of action figures as payment – for my grandson who loved playing with them. I didn't expect to receive anything, but two weeks later a box of action figures arrived in the mail. My grandson was delighted.

Incidentally, I'm not a fan of low-profile tires; my solution to their problems is to avoid them.

- Several models of Mercedes-Benz use separate sets of bolts for regular and spare tire rims. Without the special bolts for the spare, the spare rim will not mount. I first encountered this problem with a motorist on I-20 near Atlanta, whom I could not help; when I got home I went to a Mercedes-Benz dealer and learned about the special bolts for the spare.

- No convenient source of light to illuminate the area if the problem occurs at night; changing a tire in pitch darkness is challenging and slow.

Solutions to Common Tire-related Issues

The rest of this chapter will cover simple, inexpensive measures to overcome all these tire-related issues. The measures include becoming aware, planning ahead, and stowing certain items in your vehicle. The items I recommend here are many fewer than what I carry, which fit easily in the trunk of my Honda Accord. Think of them as ideas for presents for birthdays or Christmas.

Tire Care. Here is the most important sentence in this book: **The single most important way to prevent breaking down is to take care of your tires.**

Have all tires checked for wear and balancing every 5,000 miles. Tire professionals can determine whether tires are wearing evenly and safely, and check for the presence of dry rot. At least monthly, and before any trips, check the pounds per square inch (psi) air pressure in your vehicle's tires rolling on the pavement; tire underinflation is the primary cause for tire blowouts on the highway, since it causes sidewalls to flex excessively, wear out, and fail. Develop the habit of checking your tires visually each time you get in the vehicle.

Air Pressure. Correct air pressure in pounds per square inch (psi) for all tires is usually noted on a decal located just inside the driver's door jamb.

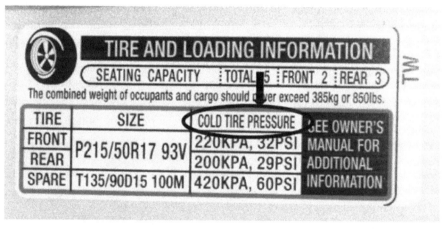

Critical tire pressure information is on decal found on driver's door jamb. Note that pressures are for "cold" tires. Correct pressures for front and rear tires may differ, as in this example. Also, required pressure for the spare tire for this vehicle, a "space saver" donut, is 60 psi.

Modern automobile tires, especially those with low profile, can appear properly inflated when they are not. Accurate readings require a tire pressure gauge. Mushy handling of a moving vehicle most often is due to underinflated tires.

18 psi: UNSAFE   36 psi: safe

These tire inflation checks alone will cut in half your chances of having a breakdown.

<u>Walt Recommends:</u> Keep a tire pressure gauge and a 12-volt air compressor in the car and <u>use them</u>. Correct pressure for most automobile tires falls in the range of 28 - 36 psi when tires are "cold" – in the morning after no driving for three hours and before driving one mile (tires driven at highway speed for 20 minutes can cause a 4-5 psi increase). Some heavy duty pickups and vans, and some trailers, use tires requiring pressures considerably higher than 60 psi. Most tires will lose 1-2 psi per month whether the tire is being used or not. I use extensively my 12-volt air compressor and tire pressure gauge.

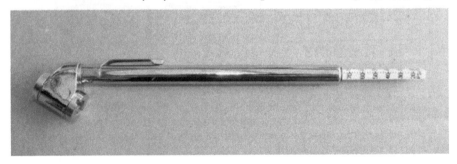

Tire pressure gauge should register pressures as high as your tires require: many new passenger vehicles use a donut (space saver) spare which will not perform safely unless inflated fully to 60 psi.

12-volt air compressor, on left ($40-$50), powered by portable jumper battery ($75-$80), and tire pressure gauge ($5): Priceless. Some air compressors come with their own power source.

NOTES:

- Portable jumper batteries, extremely useful for jump-starting engines with weak batteries and powering 12-volt air compressors (and cell phones with dead batteries), require re-charging after each use and monthly without use; otherwise, if they lose their charge, the battery will die permanently.

- Actual "cold" tire pressure varies with outside air temperature. Rule of thumb: for each increase in outside air temperature of 10 degrees Fahrenheit, actual cold tire pressure will increase 1 pound per square inch (psi), and vice versa. So, as seasons change, with significant temperature changes, the actual cold psi in your tires may require adjustment to match the "recommended" cold psi. For example: Tire pressure initially is at the correct 32 psi. When outside air temperature increases from 50 degrees to 80 degrees Fahrenheit, actual cold tire pressure will increase 3 psi (to 35 psi, which is higher than the correct level). To drive with tires at correct cold pressure, release air (in the morning before driving, while still cold) to reduce pressure by 3 psi, back to 32 psi. Do the reverse if outside air temperature decreases significantly.

Temporary Repair of a Flat Tire. Tire sealant, liquid from a pressurized can, will seal a nail hole and other slow leaks. This method also can inflate a flat spare tire if no air compressor is available. I don't use it because of its mess. Some tire warranties are voided after use of such sealants, although its use apparently does not damage the tire. Following an injection of liquid sealant, the vehicle must be driven right away in order to distribute the liquid evenly inside the tire to seal leaks and prevent tire imbalance. Also, after it has cured and hardened the sealant can make later removal of a tire from its rim (desirable in order to apply a permanent repair patch) more difficult, resulting in additional expense.

I have plugged many tires with holes in treads (holes in sidewalls are not repairable) due to nails or screws (including motorcycle tires, since there was no spare tire). The price for a plug kit is very low (I got mine at Walmart for about $10, with extra plugs). Both liquid sealants and tire plugs are temporary fix options for tires – preferably those which have become flat while sitting or which have not been driven on while flat. A major tire chain refused to fix a leaking tire of mine which I had pumped up at home and driven to their shop, because the tire had been driven for a short distance when it was flat. The store manager ruled that since the rim had been driven directly on the flat sidewall, the sidewall had been damaged, and the tire was no longer safe.

Almost all of my assists are out on the highway. I estimate that at least 70% of the flat tires I have seen there have blown out and/or shredded; these tires simply lack the structural integrity to benefit from liquid sealant or a plug job. Almost all the other flat tires I have seen on the highway have been driven some distance, at high speed, while flat with direct rim-on-sidewall contact where the rim is creasing or cutting the sidewall's structural material, rendering the tire unsafe – which neither sealant nor a plug can remedy. The times I have plugged car tires on the highway have been when the motorist has had no spare, or the spare is in horrible condition, and there was no other alternative except to call for an expensive tow which the motorist could not afford.

A tire plug kit consists of two hand instruments: a reamer to clean out and roughen up the nail hole (after extracting the nail, or screw, with pliers), and a device like a huge sewing needle with a slotted eye on its business end to draw a worm-like gooey plug in through the hole before yanking upward, leaving part of the plug inside the tire; then the portion of the plug outside the tire is trimmed with a knife. I did a plug job for a work colleague a couple of years ago when he found his car, without a spare tire, with a flat tire in the company parking lot. Of course, to find the nail/screw hole, one normally first must remove the wheel from the vehicle to check the tread. If the hole cannot be found easily, add compressed air to the leaky tire and spray soapy water to the tread and look for soap bubbles.

The permanent fix, instead of liquid sealant or a plug, is to have a tire shop remove the tire from the rim and seal the leak with a patch inside the tire. I have used plugs to fix 2 or 3 motorcycle tires out on the interstate (liquid sealant is not to be used on motorcycle tires).

Walt Recommends: Take a (temporarily) repaired flat tire immediately to a tire shop for inspection and permanent repair – most likely with a patch on the inside of the tire. I have read stories of temporary fixes' lasting a long time, but I would not bet on it. Walmart charges $10 to fix a flat tire correctly, well worth it.

Changing a Flat Tire. Before getting into the fine points of changing a flat tire, here are the basic steps, in the correct sequence – to provide context for the discussion which will follow:

1   Stop/move the vehicle with flat tire where ground is level and firm.

2   Apply parking brake, use wheel chocks (wedges placed under a wheel to prevent its rolling), and put transmission in gear or "Park".

3   Turn on vehicle hazard warning flashers.

4   Deploy reflecting warning triangles.

5   "Break" lug nuts loose on the rim with the flat tire before jacking up vehicle; do not yet remove lug nuts.

6   Get out spare; check for correct air pressure; reflate if pressure is low.

7   Jack up vehicle just enough to get spare on.

8   Remove lug nuts, then the rim with flat tire; replace with spare and screw on lug nuts.

9   Initially do not tighten lug nuts; ensure spare tire rim is flush with vehicle wheel; then "snug" tighten lug nuts, using a "star pattern" (tighten the nuts not in sequence around the rim, but alternate lug nuts on opposite sides of the rim) to ensure the rim mounts flush with the vehicle's wheel. For example, if there are six lug nuts, tighten them in this sequence (referring to positions of numbers on a clock): 12, 6, 2, 8, 4, 10.

10 Lower vehicle; then ensure the lug nuts are tight, again using the "star pattern".

11 Stow rim with flat tire. With most large vans, pickups and SUVs, reel in the steel cable which suspended the spare tire.

12 Replace or repair the flat tire right away; another flat tire without a serviceable spare greatly complicates matters.

Protection from Getting Dirty or Wet.

Several years ago, while traveling from Houston to San Antonio to visit my father I encountered a pickup truck with flat tire on the shoulder of Interstate 10. I pulled over and asked my standard opening question, "What do you need?" I felt I had obligated myself to the assist before I realized that an earlier rain had saturated the area and I would need to get down on wet ground to position my jack. I got down anyway and promptly got soaked as I changed the tire. I was wet and clammy all that day – which was the last day that I did not have a tarp in my trunk. I have used that thin, inexpensive tarp since then some fifty times, always staying dry. I was already prepared for getting down on dry, dirty ground; I carried an old beach towel, which also protects for a short while against ants and, folded over several times, provides a nice pad for my old knees on hard ground. The towel gets a good shake-out after use.

Walt Recommends: Carry an old beach towel and a cheap tarp.

Hand Protection.

Soon after I started doing roadside assists I cut my hands handling a blown out tire, which had exposed hundreds of severed razor-sharp pieces of steel wiring. Next day I got a pair of leather work gloves. No problems since then with hands being cut.

Walt Recommends: Carry leather work gloves.

Solutions to Spare Tire Issues
"Spare tires" are a huge part of the discussion about not becoming stranded.

Spare Tire On Board? Several expensive cars, with "run flat" tires which supposedly can be driven without air at moderate speed for a short distance, are not sold with a spare tire or tire changing tools. I have seen too many BMWs and Mercedes-Benz stranded because their "run flat" tire had hit debris in the road, destroying the tire, rendering it useless. The only option then is to call for a tow, which is okay, provided the "system" works to get 1) the tow truck on site quickly, and 2) a mounted replacement tire, but not okay in out-of-the-way places during odd hours after tire stores close, generally by 6 PM. Some of these cars can be equipped with optional donut-sized spare tires and tire changing tools, but the cars have no space designated for their storage – so they're rare. In high end Mercedes-Benz diesels through model year 2013 the space for a spare is taken up by a tank for urea diesel exhaust fluid to reduce toxic emissions. I'm not a fan of vehicles without spare tires.

Whenever I encounter a broken down vehicle with a flat tire, my second question, after, "What do you need?" is "Do you have a spare tire?" Generally, an answer of "Yes" is a good sign, but not always. An answer of "No" means my assist either will not happen, except to help get a tow truck and ensure the motorist knows his accurate location; or, if I have time and inclination (and tire stores are open, with correct tire) I may take him and his flat tire to the tire store, where he has the tire repaired, or replacement tire mounted, and I return him, with new tire, to his vehicle. I have done this at least twenty times. Since chances are slim that a Good Samaritan will be there for you, it's always better to have a good spare tire!

Walt Recommends: Have a serviceable spare tire – always. After changing the flat tire, it's best to have the flat tire repaired, or replaced, immediately. Otherwise, should you have another flat tire (they seem to happen in bunches) you'll have no spare to fall back on.

In November, 2009, I was returning to Texas from a funeral in Virginia, traveling south on Interstate 85 just into South Carolina around 9:30 PM, when I spotted a disabled Honda Accord on the northbound shoulder. I exited right away, turned around, and traveled north until I saw the car, pulled over ahead of it and backed up. The driver, whose wife was in the car, told me he had a flat tire and his jack was missing; also, he said that he planned to continue driving that night. The tire change was routine, and when I finished we talked a few minutes. I advised him to not continue driving that night beyond the next motel since he would not be able to replace his flat tire until morning, he had no jack, and his spare tire was old and likely to blow out. The driver was a US Marine no longer on active duty ("Once a Marine, always a Marine"). As an Army veteran I'll admit that Marines probably have the most service pride of all. He told me he had been very worried as I backed up in the darkness – until he saw my Purple Heart license plate; he said he knew then that he would be okay. I handed him my card with phone numbers and we went our separate ways. An hour or so later I received a call from my wife; she told me that the Marine had called my home phone to report he had taken my advice and checked into a motel. A few days later I received a really nice thank you note in the mail from the Marine; he also wrote, "I never thought I'd say this, but GO ARMY".

It's not uncommon for folks towing trailers to opt to travel without a spare tire for the trailer (including rentals like U-Haul) – with predictable consequences.

Walt Recommends: With trailers, carry more than one spare tire. Trailers tend to have more flat tires than motor vehicles. I have encountered several folks pulling trailers who saved themselves by stowing two or more spare tires for their trailers; others, who had only one spare, found themselves in trouble.

An answer of "Yes" to the spare tire question invites further investigation:

- **Can the Spare Tire be Made Available for Use?** Most spares for
  sedans are in the trunk and easily accessible, unless the wing nut securing the spare to the trunk floor is corroded, in which case you'll need
  pliers or vise-grips to loosen the wing nut. Most spares for minivans are
  located either under the front seats or midway to the second row of seats.
  Some minivans' spares are accessible inside the vehicle under a floor cover; others are lowered beneath the vehicle by cable activated by turning a
  bolt on the floor between the front seats or behind the front seats. SUV
  spare carry configuration varies considerably. Some SUVs mount their
  spares outside on the back of the vehicle or inside the vehicle, upright,
  above the rear floor. Some spares are inside the SUV beneath the rear
  floor, accessible by hand; others are beneath the vehicle just forward of
  the rear bumper, lowered either by turning a bolt on the rear floor or by
  turning a shaft inserted through the back of the vehicle – usually near or
  through the rear bumper. I have encountered a handful of SUVs whose
  shaft access hole was blocked because the vehicle's rear door or hatchback
  could not be opened.

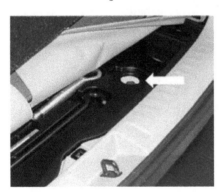 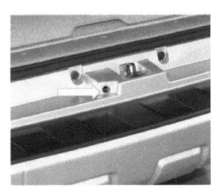

Bolt to lower the spare of
Toyota 4-Runner is on rear
floorboard inside the vehicle.

Access hole for shaft to lower the
spare of this Toyota Highlander
is just above rear bumper, con-
cealed by a closed hatchback.

Such was the case in Texas with "Joseph", a very large man from Cameroon. His Toyota Highlander was stopped on the shoulder of Interstate 10; its right front tire was flat. Its occupants were roasting on the hot summer day. Joseph, the driver and father of the family, told me that he couldn't get to his spare tire because the vehicle's rear hatchback, which covered access to lower the spare, wouldn't open. So, I jacked up his vehicle, removed the flat tire, wrapped it in an old sheet, and put it in my car. Joseph and I took it to a Walmart for repair (all it needed was a valve stem). We returned to his vehicle, where I remounted the repaired tire. His 8-year old twin daughters, coached and rehearsed while Joseph and I were gone, performed a really cute, lively "Thank You" dance for me. Very nice. Before I departed, I suggested Joseph visit the nearby Toyota dealer to fix the latch on his rear door; he declined, saying he was in a hurry. His wife remarked acidly, "We might as well not have a spare tire". I decided to leave before their fight!

Spare tires for most large SUVs, vans and pickups are under the vehicle's back deck, lowered and raised by a cable activated by a sectioned shaft which is inserted through a hole near or in the bumper and a plastic guide tube, to engage a lowering mechanism just above the spare tire. One key to success is to use the correct configuration of the "business end" of the shaft which engages the lowering mechanism. Generally, GM vehicles use an open square which slides over a slightly smaller square tit; whereas generally, Ford and Toyota vehicles use a prong which slides into a slot. Nissan uses a T-fitting which slides into their uniquely-shaped slot. I have found exceptions to all of this. When in doubt consult the pictures in the owner's manual!

<u>The important point here is that you need to know how to access your vehicle's spare tire, and you should practice doing that before your vehicle breaks down out on the interstate.</u> Get out the owner's manual, read it, and then practice using the vehicle's tools to get the spare out. Rehearsing this with your "significant other" on a nice day in your driveway can save immense anxiety later. Some vehicles have a lock to prevent theft of the spare tire; if yours does, being able to find and use the key to unlock the lock is very useful. Keep the key in the vehicle where you can find it, say with your tire changing tools. I have found that these keys, like a lost contact lens, usually can be found with a thorough search.

- **Is the Spare Tire Rim the Correct One for the Vehicle?** If you are certain that your spare is the one which came with the vehicle when it was new, the answer is "yes". I have encountered at least twenty-five cases where the spare rim was not the original, and it would not fit properly on the vehicle's wheel.

The Chrysler minivan was on the shoulder of Interstate 10 in Katy, Texas, with a flat left front tire. A man and two women were out of the van standing next to the concrete divider. The man was striking the divider with what looked like the vehicle's jack which appeared broken. Heavy traffic rushing by was loud, making verbal communication difficult.

When I asked, "What do you need?" the man pointed to his flat tire. He had already gotten out his spare, which I checked and found to be flat. So, I started to reflate it with my 12-volt air compressor as I jacked up the vehicle using my jack and removed the rim with flat tire. When I tried to mount his inflated spare tire, its rim would not fit flush with the vehicle's wheel, although the vehicle's wheel had five lugs and the rim for the spare had five holes to mate with the lugs. I turned to the man to describe the problem, and saw that he was "signing" with the women; no wonder he and I had difficulty conversing! The loud traffic didn't help, but it wouldn't have made any difference. He could read my lips, but he couldn't speak clearly to me. I found a paper tablet and pen which we then used to communicate.

He wrote down that he had bought the flat tire at a Discount Tire store. I wrapped his flat tire with rim in a plastic bag and put it in my car. The man and I drove to a nearby Discount Tire store, arriving one minute before closing time. I explained to the manager the situation; he confirmed by computer that the man's tire was a Discount Tire purchase. The big-hearted manager replaced the flat tire with a new one and rebalanced the wheel – for free (kudos to that manager and Discount Tire). We returned to the disabled van and mounted the rim with new tire. All the folks with the minivan were ecstatic. Before the man and his friends left I reminded him to get the proper rim for his spare tire. Done. A very good day!

Walt Recommends: If you are not certain whether your spare tire is original equipment, take your vehicle to a tire shop and check the fit of your spare tire's rim; or do it yourself. It's best to ensure that the mounted spare rim with tire will turn freely without any rubbing once the lug nuts are tightened.

- **Is the Spare Tire Fully Inflated?** <u>80%</u> of spare tires I see are either totally out of air or have much too little to perform safely without being reflated. Since 75% of my assists involve a tire issue, this means that fully 60% of all my assists involve a very low or flat spare tire!

> On a trip on I-40 to Raleigh, NC, I encountered, within a span of 15 minutes, three vehicles with flat tires; in all three cases the spare tires were either very low on air or flat.

Most tires will lose 1-2 psi per month whether the tire is being used or not. Most donut spares require 60 psi to function safely. Best to check psi with a tire pressure gauge (you need a gauge that goes up to at least 60 psi; not all do). Countless times the stranded motorist has thumped the spare with a finger or fist and declared it "full"; then I'll suggest we "just check" with the tire pressure gauge, and the spare will almost always be empty or nearly so. Then I inflate the tire using my 12-volt air compressor, powered either from a cigarette lighter receptacle or a 12-volt receptacle on my portable jumper battery. After a spare tire has gone unused a long time, especially after hanging under a vehicle and exposed to the elements, chances are it will be flat; when this happens the airtight seal between the tire and rim has likely failed – preventing the tire from accepting and retaining compressed air, and rendering the spare useless. I have been lucky several times; my compressor was powerful enough to cause the bead to re-seal with a loud, "Pop Pop Pop".

Walt Recommends: Physically check the spare for air pressure, with tire pressure gauge, every six months, and for certain before a trip. Identifying the location of leaks is made easy by applying soapy water and looking for bubbles; I keep a small spray bottle of soapy water in my trunk.

- **Is the Spare Tire in Good Condition, Safe for Use?** If your spare has been used, ask your tire dealer to inspect its condition. It's a good idea to have that tire balanced (especially a used full-sized spare) so it doesn't vibrate when it rolls.

- **How Old is the Spare Tire?** For tires manufactured in 2000 or later there will be four numbers in the last cluster of the DOT number on a tire's sidewall, which tell week and year of manufacture: for example, "0511" indicates the tire was manufactured the 5th week of 2011. Tires manufactured before 2000 will have three numbers; "309" would mean the tire was manufactured in the 30th week of either 1999 or 1989 (in either case, much too old to be safe).

DOT number on tire sidewall shows week and year of manufacture, here: 5th week, 2011.

Opinions among tire professionals vary as to when a tire, <u>spare or otherwise</u>, should be replaced due to age. Michelin will not warranty its tires after six years and recommends replacement at ten years. Goodyear places no age limits, suggesting close inspection for cracking in sidewalls (I would have this inspection done at a tire shop). Several tire experts, however, recommend replacement at six years.

<u>Walt Recommends:</u> After digesting lots of information and seeing many blown out old tires, I say <u>get rid of all tires, even unused spares, after six years.</u> Old tires seem to be especially common on trailers and campers, which typically are not used constantly. Most often when a motor vehicle is pulling a trailer and there is a flat tire, the flat tire is on the trailer. I have changed at least one hundred flat trailer tires; almost all were much older than six years. Tires on trailers and campers also tend to go flat due to typically long periods without use and constant exposure to sunlight, factors which accelerate tire aging – the same factors which accelerate aging in people.

Enough on spare tires. Whether you pay attention to the spare tire issues above and take steps to address them likely will determine whether you become stranded should you have a flat tire.

Solutions to Typical Problems Removing and Mounting Tires

Fundamental tasks when you have a flat tire: Loosening, removing, and (once the spare is ready for mounting) replacing the lug nuts which hold the rim to the vehicle's wheel. This discussion applies also to European cars (Mercedes-Benz, BMW, Audi, some Volkswagens) which use bolts instead of lugs and lug nuts, and to trailers, whose wheels often have lug nuts of different size and configuration from the towing vehicle.

Capability to Loosen Lug Nuts/Bolts. Removing and replacing lug nuts normally requires the lug wrench which comes with the vehicle, typically a sturdy steel rod, bent almost 90 degrees, with an open head on one end and handle on the other.

Handles on most vehicle-issued lug wrenches are too short to gain sufficient leverage to "break" (loosen) really tight lug nuts.

The wrench's head is designed to grasp the lug nut. The relatively short handles of most vehicle-issued lug wrenches often do not provide sufficient leverage to "break" (loosen) lug nuts on a flat tire rim. Some folks try to stand on the lug wrench handle when it is horizontal to generate increased leverage; however, this can be dangerous since chances of feet slipping off the handle or lug wrench head popping off the lug nut (or bolt with many German cars) are good. A much better solution: 1) Tell your tire shop to not over-tighten your vehicle's lug nuts; 2) Get a "4-way" lug wrench (at least 22 inches across) for extra leverage and speed with lug nuts; and/or 3) Get a "cheater bar", a 2-feet long steel pipe, 1 inch in diameter, which can be slipped over the handle of your vehicle's lug wrench to double or triple available leverage. No lug nut or bolt can withstand the torque from a cheater bar; I have sheared off lugs when the lug nut was frozen and absolutely would not unscrew. Application of some "Liquid Wrench" or "PB Blaster" spray to the lug nut before trying to loosen it also helps.

Cheater bar slipped over end of a lug wrench provides much more leverage than lug wrench alone. This method is much safer than standing on a horizontal lug wrench handle.

"4-way" lug wrench provides superior leverage and speed when removing and replacing lug nuts. Here, the 4-way is used to "spin" off loosened lug nuts, as she flicks upward on the right side and the wrench rotates in her left hand.

New vehicles will likely have all required tire-changing tools, including lug wrench. Many older vehicles, however, for a variety of reasons, lack some required tire-changing tools.

Aftermarket Rims: Lug Wrench May Not Work. It seems like many vehicles on the highway use aftermarket rims. More often than not, neither the vehicle's stock lug wrench nor most 4-way lug wrenches will fit into the opening around the lug nut. This is a very common problem.

Tight gap between lug nut and edge of the hole in this rim will not permit use of lug wrench.

Tight gap between lug nut and inside of its hole in the rim, common with after-market rims.

Compare thick wall around lug wrench head (left), with thin wall of same-size ½-inch drive socket (right). Lug wrench head will not fit in gap between lug nut and hole. <u>The socket will fit.</u>

The best solution in this situation is to use a properly sized ½-inch drive socket (whose walls are thinner than the lug wrench's head) in conjunction with an extension bar and a ½-inch drive ratchet wrench or breaker bar.

<u>Walt Recommends:</u> Determine <u>before</u> having a flat tire, what will be required to loosen your vehicle's lug nuts (any reputable auto parts store can help determine the correct size socket); then acquire needed items and practice with them. No need here to remove any lug nuts. Just ensure that you can "break" loose each of them one at a time; then re-tighten each (tight, but not super-tight) before "breaking" the next one.

Rounded Lug Nuts. Too often I encounter lug nuts whose outer edges have become "rounded" from previous improper use of pliers, vise grips, or incorrect size wrench or socket. You will not need any special tools as long as your lug nuts are not rounded.

<u>Walt Recommends:</u> Either inspect the lug nuts yourself or ask your tire shop to, and replace any lug nuts that are rounded. Then be sure to use the correct size lug wrench head, or socket (not too large), when loosening or tightening your lug nuts.

Wheel Locks (also known as "Locking Lug Nuts"). Many vehicles have locks on their rims to prevent theft. The lock on each rim replaces one of the lug nuts. If you have the key unique to the set of four locks for the vehicle's wheels, you'll have no worries about unlocking a wheel lock when that tire goes flat.

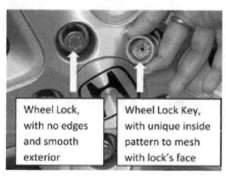

Wheel lock and wheel lock key

Wheel lock key fitted on wheel lock. Lug wrench fits over key as if it were a lug nut.

Without this key, there will be big problems until I or another Good Samaritan comes along with "special tools" to defeat the lock.

This is exactly what happened in late 2009 on Interstate 10 near Houston, when I encountered the vice president of a large bank. His Infiniti's right rear tire was flat, and he could not find the key to his locking lug nut. We searched his car for the key, to no avail. So, out came my "special tool" ½-inch drive socket with its inside-the-head hardened steel twists which grabbed and bit into the outside of his locking lug nut, eventually with enough force to unscrew it. He invited me to lunch the following weekend (where he told me he had later found the missing key wedged among some papers in his car), and we became friends; we still occasionally exchange emails.

Walt Recommends: Ensure you can find your vehicle's key to the locks on its four rims. The "lost contact lens" analogy fits here too, in case you cannot find the key right away: Keep searching.

Requirement for Deep Socket. Occasionally, I have encountered situations, mostly on heavy duty vans or pickups, where the wheel lugs protrude so far out from the lug nut that a standard lug wrench head or socket is not deep enough to fit over the length of the lug and grab the lug nut.

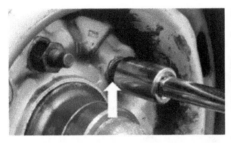

Standard socket is not deep enough to fit all the way over lug nut with protruding lug. Result: insufficient grip.

Deep socket is required to accommodate protruding lug and achieve sufficient grip on lug nut.

After this happened the first time I invested in some deep sockets, which have worked fine ever since.

Walt Recommends: If you drive a heavy duty van or pickup, check for protruding wheel lugs and whether your wrench or socket will reach the lug nuts. Whereas I stock many different socket sizes, you need only to have one: in the correct size for your vehicle's lug nuts.

Extension Bar for "Standoff" Situations. Some rims, including those for dual wheel pickups, trailers, and campers, as well as their spare tire rims, have a "deep dish" shape with lug nuts recessed from the rim's edge, which makes applying force with a ½-inch drive socket impossible without an extension bar between the wrench and socket. After my first encounter with this, I got a 10-inch extension bar, which solved that problem. A rim need not be "deep dish" to require an extension bar; I use a 2- or 4-inch extension bar when I work with lug nuts on standard rims. Extension bars can be fitted end-to-end, if needed, for additional "standoff". Routinely, I use with my extension bars a "breaker bar" (at least 18 inches long) to "break" loose tight lug nuts. A cheater bar slipped over a breaker bar, same as with a lug wrench as described earlier, provides extra leverage no stuck lug nut can resist. A ½-inch drive ratchet wrench may be used for this, but these wrenches may become damaged under a heavy load.

An "extension bar" provides access to lug nuts recessed from the edge of the rim. A "breaker bar" along with extension bar is the best way to achieve leverage to loosen tight lug nuts. For additional leverage, use a cheater bar in conjunction with breaker bar.

Removal (and Replacement) of Loosened Lug Nuts.
Lug nuts (or bolts, for many German cars) loosened with ½-inch drive socket are most quickly unscrewed and removed (and later replaced and screwed back on) by using an old-fashion, low-tech ½-inch drive "speed wrench". This works especially well where lug nuts (or bolts) fit in holes that are deeply recessed and not accessible by your fingers; also when a 4-way lug wrench will not work. A ½-inch drive ratchet wrench can be used for this, but the speed wrench is much faster. I bought mine on eBay for $19.

Low tech "speed wrench" provides a simple, cheap and quick way to unscrew and remove loosened lug nuts. It works just as well in reverse when screwing on and replacing the nuts until they are snug while mounting the spare tire. Using an extension bar between the speed wrench and the socket (such a configuration is not shown above) makes unscrewing (and screwing on) lug nuts more comfortable while sitting on the ground facing the wheel. Then use a breaker bar to retighten snug lug nuts.

Walt Recommends: Check your vehicle's wheels for rims with "deep dish" shape where lug nuts are recessed from the rim's edge; if so, get an extension bar and a breaker bar. Extension bars usually become "must have" items whenever using a ½-inch drive wrench and sockets, since they lessen chances of "knuckles scraping fender" during "breaking", loosening, and tightening of lug nuts and bolts.

Some aftermarket rims include a cap over the lug nuts – for security and/or flashy appearance. This cap is held in place with several hexnuts, which require the correctly sized hex wrench for removal and replacement.

Some fancy aftermarket wheels require a hex wrench to remove cap which secures access to lug nuts

Removal of Rim Stuck to Vehicle Wheel. Occasionally, I have removed a wheel's lug nuts, but the rim remained stuck to the vehicle wheel and could not be pulled off by hand.

The Mazda 626 belonging to the elderly man on Interstate 10 near Brookshire, Texas, had had a blowout. He had moved it to a wide shoulder, jacked it up, and removed the lug nuts, but he was in tears of frustration. He had been there for hours because the rim with flat tire was stuck to his car. I checked his spare tire which was very low on air. As my compressor pumped air into his spare, I tried unsuccessfully with my hands to remove the flat tire's rim from his car. Then I remembered that I had a hammer in my trunk. With the hammer I struck the inside metal part of his rim a couple of times, and the rim dislodged and fell away from the car. The old man was delirious with relief, giving me a 10-second bear hug as traffic zoomed by at 80 mph. We soon mounted his inflated spare on the car, and he requested my business card. A couple of hours later he called my house and thanked me again; then his wife did the same. Just after this assist I obtained a steel-headed mallet, which I have used the same way at least twenty-five times.

The culprit was rust which formed because the rims had not been taken off the wheels in a long time. My preferred solution is to use my mallet to strike the side of the rim in contact with the vehicle's wheel; normally a mild hit will do the trick. This technique will not damage the rim. An alternative solution to loosen the rim is to replace the lug nuts "finger tight", lower the vehicle, and rock the vehicle.

Walt Recommends: Have your vehicle's tires inspected, rotated and balanced every 5,000 miles – which also will ensure that your rims do not stay mounted on the vehicle's wheels long enough to become stuck on with rust.

Likely I have told you more than you would have imagined for issues removing and replacing rims. You would be wise to follow my advice, to avoid becoming stranded. As you can see, this is not rocket science. Instead it's all about awareness, common sense, and making the effort to prevent problems and fix things <u>before</u> the flat tire.

Solutions to Typical Problems with Vehicle Jacks

Proper Jack and Lift Points for your Vehicle. As with the lug wrench, if your vehicle has a jack and you are certain that it is the one which came with the vehicle when it was new, cause for worry is remote. Very often, however, I find that the vehicle has no jack, an incomplete jack, or the jack is from another vehicle and it will not work.

<u>**Walt Recommends:**</u> Compare jack components with those listed in the owner's manual to ensure that you have them all (or have a car dealer do this). Different types of vehicles come with different types and sizes of jacks. You will be in infinitely better shape when you actually have a flat tire if you take the time and effort <u>before the flat</u> to ensure you have the correct jack, can operate it, and know the proper vehicle lift points.

Lift points for most sedans and minivans. Look for small sections of reinforced steel, front and rear, just inside the lower edge of the vehicle's body.

Lift point for pickup/van back wheel: directly on the round axle, near the wheel with flat tire

Lift point for pickup/van front wheel: directly on the underside of the frame member just behind the wheel with flat tire

Using improper lift points can damage your vehicle and cause the vehicle to fall off the jack. Conversely, using correct lift points makes use of a good jack quite safe. Lift point for changing a rear tire on large pickups, vans and SUVs generally is the rear axle (or with independent rear suspensions, a point there near the wheel), not the frame; reason: excessive play in the rear suspension requires considerably higher elevation of the frame to get the rear wheel off the ground. In any case, consult the owner's manual!

Jack Stability. The second greatest risk (after being hit by another vehicle) during a tire change is the vehicle's rolling off the jack – during lifting and once jacked up. Several times I have seen vehicles which have rolled while being jacked up, falling off the jack and wedging the jack under the vehicle. If the vehicle rolls after it has been jacked up and flat tire removed, the problems can be greater: possible injury to the person changing the tire; and the vehicle wheel, without a rim, ends up on the ground, too low to fit the jack again under the vehicle. Before starting to jack up a vehicle I always ask the driver, "Is your parking brake on?"

Walt Recommends: Always, and especially when the vehicle is on a downhill or uphill slope, ensure that the vehicle's parking brake is on and either the vehicle's automatic transmission is in "Park", or its manual transmission is in first gear or reverse, before jacking up the vehicle. In addition, place chock blocks under wheel diagonally opposite the one with flat tire.

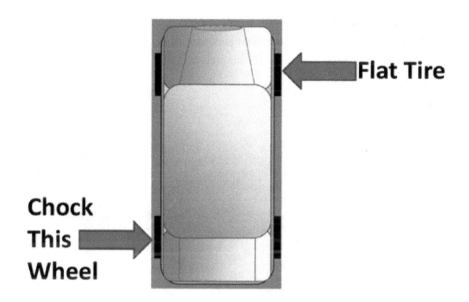

Flat Tire

Chock This Wheel

Wheel chocks prevent vehicle from rolling. Best to also use vehicle's parking brake and place transmission in "Park" or 1st gear/reverse gear.

Most vehicle jacks perform well when the ground is hard and even, but not so well when the ground is sandy, soft, mushy, covered with vegetation, or uneven – then jacks will sink and become unstable. Unfortunately, you'll not be able to choose where you have that flat tire. The bottom surface area of most jacks is too small to prevent sinking or tilting in these situations.

Walt Recommends: Stow with your tools a piece of treated plywood board 8" X 8"X ½" thick to place under your jack to redistribute the vehicle's weight on soft ground or sand, to stabilize the jack and prevent it from sinking.

Piece of ½-inch treated plywood under the jack prevents jack from sinking in soft ground.

On the shoulder of Interstate 10 in Texas was a Mercedes-Benz sports car with a flat right front tire. The right wheels were just off the hard shoulder on soft grassy soil. Another motorist had stopped to help and, using the Mercedes' jack, had raised the vehicle high enough to remove the rim with the flat tire. The problem was that the small base of the car's jack had then sunk into the soil so far that the front brake disk was on the ground and sinking farther – too low to permit mounting the vehicle's spare tire. My hydraulic jack, designed for low profile lifts like this (with 3 inches of clearance) worked perfectly, with my sheet metal strips underneath the jack's wheels to prevent their sinking in the soil or snagging on divots in the ground. I jacked up the car and completed the tire change without difficulty. The driver was very relieved and asked me for my mailing address so she could send me a thank-you note.

After the assist and I had driven away, it occurred to me that this situation could have been prevented if the driver had had a stiff, strong flat surface to place under the vehicle's jack to distribute the car's weight over a greater area than the jack's small base. I went to a hardware store and asked one of the managers what he recommended for material to cut into squares 8" X 8"; his answer: ½-inch treated plywood. So, I bought a few small sheets of that material and cut it into squares at home with a power saw. From the thank-you note I knew the mailing address of the driver. I wrote with black magic marker on one side of one of the squares, "PLACE UNDER VEHICLE JACK WHEN GROUND IS SOFT", and I mailed it to her. Since then I have made hundreds of these squares and given them to friends and some of my assist recipients. I always keep a small stash in my car trunk, and a larger number in my garage at home – where my wife just loves to find space for them! Incidentally, the driver turned out to be a well-known TV personality who, years later, arranged and did a short TV segment with me on a Houston station.

Another factor with jack stability, to prevent a vehicle from slipping off its jack, is to ensure that the lift will be vertical (to counter gravity, which is also vertical) – often not a simple matter if the car is stopped where its right wheels are significantly lower than its left wheels (or vice versa) such as on a steeply sloping highway shoulder. If possible, move the vehicle to a more level location nearby to minimize left-right cant. To further secure a level base for my jack so it lifts vertically and not at an angle, I use extra pieces from my stash of 8"X8"X ½" pieces of treated plywood as shoring under my jack.

Walt Recommends: If the vehicle with flat tire is on a significant left-right cant, relocate the vehicle to the most level spot nearby which also is safe from oncoming traffic. Ensure the jack lifts vertically, not at an angle.

Jacks for Trailers. Motor vehicle jacks do not always work when a towed trailer has a flat tire. Configurations of trailer undercarriages differ so much that the driver needs to assess his trailer's lift requirements and, if necessary, obtain a separate jack, and tools, for the trailer. I have found that successful lifting of trailers often requires performing the task in stages: using a jack stand in order to maintain initial lift while repositioning the jack to a then-more accessible, better lift point (most often the axle) in order to achieve enough height to remove the flat tire and mount the spare. Placing lumber under the jack and jack stand for added elevation (for example, between lift stages) often is key to success.

Often, when trailers use two tandem wheels on a side, both wheels can be elevated simultaneously by moving the trailer either forward or backward, rolling the wheel without flat tire up a ramp (with a flat surface on top for the good wheel), perhaps improvised from lumber – making a jack unnecessary.

Walt Recommends: Ensure you have a jack suitable for the trailer. Also advisable to have: jack stand, and lumber for jack stability and necessary elevation. Have a ramp, with flat section at the top, for trailers with tandem wheels.

Maneuvering Tires

The thought of having to handle and lift heavy tires can intimidate. However, lifting a tire is not necessary. Instead, plan to drag a spare tire a very short distance (say from under a van, once the spare is lowered with lots of extra lift cable let out; or drive the vehicle forward a couple of feet to expose the tire), tilt and remove the cable's retaining bracket from the center of the spare, tilt the spare tire from horizontal to upright so it can be rolled, and then roll the tire over to the vehicle wheel for mounting.

Spare tire at end of extended cable – Lower, then drag spare back, or drive forward 1-2 feet to expose tire, <u>before</u> removing lug nuts or rim with flat tire from vehicle.

Tilt retainer bracket; lift through center of rim

The vehicle should be jacked up just high enough to permit removing the flat tire and mounting the spare after lining up the rim's lug holes with the wheel's lugs. The act of lifting the spare rim the last ¼ inch so that the wheel's lugs align with and pass through the rim's lug holes can be made easier by using the cheater bar as a lever under the spare, lifting the tire by grasping the other end of the cheater bar.

Use cheater bar as lever to lift spare tire the last ¼ inch on to vehicle wheel so the wheel lugs mate with the holes in the rim.

Spacers

With some aftermarket rims, a spacer is needed between the rim and the vehicle's wheel to provide offset and ensure a correct fit. If the aftermarket rim is removed with the flat tire, and an original equipment rim is used as a spare, the spare will not seat correctly on the vehicle wheel unless the spacer is removed. I encountered this situation with a Volkswagen Passat on a freeway near Baltimore; I had to remove the spacer by prying it from the vehicle's wheel with a large screwdriver.

Changing a Tire at Night

Imagine having to change a tire at night. Changing a tire in pitch darkness is challenging and slow. It's much easier and quicker with a convenient source of light to illuminate your work. Many portable jumper batteries have a small, bright lamp which can be trained on the wheel and your work. A flashlight works best when someone else can hold it for the tire changer. Best solution I have found, and have used several times, is a headlamp, which requires no one else to hold and can be aimed effortlessly exactly where you need light.

The headlamp is the most efficient form of lighting for working in darkness: the required light follows the user's head and eyes, without requirement for someone else to hold the light.

Walt Recommends: Have a source of light for night work. Remember to have fresh batteries.

Here's an extract from my recent column in The Fayetteville Observer newspaper which captures many points regarding tire-related issues:

On Thanksgiving Day, 2016, I stopped on Interstate 95 for a late model white Chevrolet Equinox SUV on the inside median. I pulled up even with it on the right shoulder and saw that its right front tire was flat; both right wheels were less than three feet from the left drive lane. When traffic allowed, I walked across the drive lanes and asked, "Would you like some help with that flat tire?" The driver was a young lady about 19 traveling from Fayetteville to Raleigh. She said she had been there about an hour and had called her commercial roadside assist service, which told her they would be there in 3-4 hours. I told her I could change the tire quickly but we would need to move the SUV across to the right shoulder, which was fairly wide and where I would be much safer from oncoming traffic. She asked me to move her vehicle there, which I did. The SUV then was canted a bit to the right since its right tires were on grass and a few inches lower than the left tires, so I shored up the downhill end of the piece of lumber placed under my hydraulic jack – to ensure a horizontal base for the jack, and a vertical jack-up. Four of the lug nuts game loose with my 4-way, but I had to use my heavy artillery (socket, extension bar, breaker bar, and cheater bar) to loosen the fifth. Her compact spare had only 35 psi, so my 12-volt compressor reflated it to its required 60 psi. I asked her to apply her parking brake, and I chocked the left rear tire so the SUV would not roll. She said that the flat tire had a bolt in its tread. I asked her how she knew that, and she replied that she knew it before she began her trip, but a friend told her not to worry. I told her that she had received some bad advice. Besides driving knowing her tire had a bolt in it, she told me the reason she had stopped on the median is that she was "a left lane driver" – not a good habit. Some people are still alive in spite of themselves! After removing the flat and mounting the spare I inspected the tread of the flat tire and found a place where something had been stuck in the tread. I suggested that I plug that hole and reflate the tire so she would have a spare if another tire failed – since most tire stores were closed on Thanksgiving Day. She agreed and I did that; I then sprayed soapy water on the plug: no bubbles, so the plug wasn't leaking.

Walt's Tips:

- A tire with bolt in its tread is a time bomb, even if the leak is very slow. Get it fixed right away. Do not drive it at highway speeds.

- "A left lane driver"? Not a good idea unless passing. Even so, it's usually much safer to stop on the wider right shoulder in an emergency.

- If you must jack up a tilted vehicle, ensure that the base of the jack is horizontal, for a safe vertical lift.

- A 2-foot long steel pipe used as cheater bar will permit anyone to loosen extra-tight lug nuts.

Chapter Summary:

1. Huge preventive measure for all tire-related issues: take care of your tires: buy quality; have them inspected, rotated and balanced every 5,000 miles.

2. Pay special attention to your spare tire: correct size; inflated; good condition; less than six years old; accessible.

3. Get tools needed to jack up your vehicle and remove tires; practice accessing spare and changing a tire before "show time".

4. Have lumber (8"X8"X ½" treated plywood) to place under your jack if ground is soft.

5. May need to move the vehicle with flat tire slightly to ensure your jack has a firm, level base to permit vertical lifting.

6. Prevent the vehicle from rolling during jack-up and while changing the tire: Parking brake; Chock blocks; Transmission in "Park" or 1st gear/ reverse.

7. Review the owner's manual: Procedures; Lift points; Tools

8. Plan for a night-time tire change.

9. Points 1-8 above apply to trailers also.

Chapter 4

"Out of Gas" Issues

Running Out of Gas

Let's face it: running out of gas (OOG) is humbling. It generates around 10% of my assists, and the motorists typically feel sheepish because it is so preventable. OOG assists are my easiest because usually they require only pouring gas from my can into their tank.

"Rock the Car"

After running OOG on level ground most drivers pull over to a shoulder, which often is not level – causing any newly added fuel to pool in the tank away from the intake for the fuel line to the engine. My solution, used some thirty times, almost always works: "rock the car", by jumping on the open passenger side door frame – causing the added fuel to slosh in the tank and find the intake, as the driver tries to start. Magic! Once the engine starts it's best to move the vehicle to a level surface right away so added fuel continues to reach the intake to the engine.

"Rock the Car" causes newly added fuel to slosh in the tank and find the intake to the engine.

Regular vs. Premium Gas

I encountered a brand new Lexus 470 SUV stopped on the shoulder of Interstate 10 in July; the large family had been there a while since they were all red-faced, sweaty and hot. When I pulled over, stopped and asked the driver, "What do you need?" he responded that he was out of gas. I told him I had two gallons in my trunk and asked whether he would like some. He then surprised me with his question, "Is it Premium?" I told him no, it was regular, but his engine would run okay on regular for the short distance (about ½ mile) to the next exit where he could top off with premium. He hemmed and hawed and then said his brother was bringing some premium gas out to him. I asked, "So, you don't want any gas from me?" He replied "No, thanks", and my attempted assist was over. He and his family continued to bake.

Conclusions:

- Vehicles designed to run on premium gasoline can run on regular, especially for a short distance; the only consequence is a very slight drop in performance. Accepting regular gas in an emergency will not hurt the vehicle.

- On the other hand, I encountered a stranded motorist in a Dodge Viper whose engine had been modified to 1200 horsepower. I believed him when he declined my offer of regular gasoline, saying his engine required racing fuel.

What are the Reasons Folks Run Out of Gas?

- Driver inattention to the gauge

- Gas gauge is inaccurate

- Driver trying to squeeze out "just a few more miles" before refueling, perhaps where gas is less expensive

The best remedy is to fill up when the gauge says ¼ full (½ full is better when driving in harsh winter conditions where a vehicle could get stuck in a ditch), and not wait until the "fuel low" light comes on (it may be burned out); also, you could get caught in a traffic jam on an interstate highway. If you rely on your light, record how many gallons it takes to fill your tank just after the light comes on; then when the light comes on you can approximate gallons, and miles, remaining. For example: Owner's manual (typically on the last page under "Capacities") says gas tank capacity is 17 gallons. After a gas tank fill-up, you record total miles on the odometer (let's say 50,000). You drive around using that tank of gas and note odometer miles when the "fuel low" light comes on (say, 50,400) and immediately refill the gas tank; the tank accepts 13.5 gallons. You calculate miles per gallon as 400 miles/13.5 gallons = 29.6 mpg. You calculate that gallons remaining in the tank just before fill-up were 17 minus 13.5 = 3.5 gallons. You can estimate miles remaining (in a perfect world) as 3.5 gallons X 29.6 mpg = 103 miles. WARNING: Do not plan on driving 103 miles before running out. Always leave room for error; maybe, in a real pinch, count on driving half that calculated distance. Remember that a vehicle's fuel efficiency is almost always lower while driving around town, compared to highway driving (some hybrid cars are the exception).

If the fuel gauge is broken, get it fixed. Until then, set the trip odometer to zero at each fill-up and estimate remaining fuel and miles to go. Several times when a broken down motorist has told me he had gas and his gauge seemed to confirm so, I suspected the gauge was wrong. I added a gallon of gas, and the engine started.

NOTE: When a diesel-powered vehicle runs out of fuel getting the engine to start after adding fuel to the tank is much more difficult and involved than with a gasoline engine – beyond the scope of this book since procedures vary among vehicles (I recently made a successful such assist, but my later research revealed considerable complexities). My best advice is to ensure that a diesel vehicle does not run out of fuel! The case in point involved a borrowed diesel pickup whose owner failed to warn the borrower that the fuel gauge was broken so a user should have never let the gauge show less than ½ tank (it was at ¼ tank when the engine stopped).

Walt Recommends: Keep an empty (for safety) 1-gallon gas can in the vehicle so if you run out you can walk with it to the next exit and get gas. Or maybe a Good Samaritan will come along and give you a ride; or, if you are concerned about accepting a ride, he may drive with only your can to the next exit, fill it, and return it to your car. Highway Patrol officers normally are not allowed to carry gas in a can, but they usually will take your can to fetch gas on a case-by-case basis. (I keep a very sturdy OSHA-approved 2-gallon steel "Type 1 safety can" of gasoline, placed in a heavy plastic tub, secured in the forward section of my trunk. I do not recommend you do the same; I accept the risk since I do this routinely. I also keep funnels to prevent spills while pouring.)

Remember to "rock the car" if merely adding fuel does not work. If you are alone and the car won't start, rock the car yourself, and then start it.

Chapter Summary:

1. If your car's gas gauge is broken, get it fixed.

2. Fill up when gas level gets down to ¼ tank.

3. Carry an empty gas can in case you do run out.

4. "Rock the Car"

Chapter 5

Engine Overheating Issues

Causes of Overheating

Vehicle engine overheating can be caused by many things, some complex and beyond the scope of this book. Basic reasons for overheating include: too little coolant (normally a 50/50 antifreeze/water mix year around) in the cooling system – often caused by a leak in the system, thermostat is not functioning to permit circulation of the coolant, water pump is broken, or one or more cooling fans has stopped working. My assists address coolant level, occasional temporary mending of hoses carrying coolant, and temporary measures to restore the cooling fans. The other problems require a mechanic and spare parts, which I do not carry.

Warning Signs

Normally there will be indicators before a breakdown that there is a problem with the vehicle's cooling system, such as high readings on the engine temperature gauge, puddles of coolant (not water from the AC) under the vehicle, or steam or smoke coming out from under the hood, and/or an odor.

Preventing Overheating Breakdowns

The best way to prevent a breakdown before a trip is to act on the warning signs by taking the vehicle to a shop and have the cooling system checked and repaired by a mechanic. All of my "engine overheating" assists could have been prevented this way.

Pay attention to the engine temperature gauge! The needle should be less than half-way from "Cold" to "Hot". Otherwise, have a mechanic check the engine cooling system.

Often I find vehicles broken down with almost no coolant, and their cooling systems have taken up to two gallons of my water, enough to permit driving off the highway to a repair facility. One way to nurse an overheating engine (hopefully while being driven to a mechanic) is to turn off the air conditioner and turn up the vehicle's passenger compartment heater as hot as it will go, even in hot weather; this will help transfer heat away from the engine. Sometimes one or more aging electric cooling fans which force extra air through the radiator will stop working, usually due to the fan's electrical motor armatures' sticking. Often a gentle tap on the fan motor with a hammer (while the engine is not running) will jar loose temporarily the stuck armature. When access to the fans' motors with a hammer is restricted I have used my cheater bar to transmit the impact of the hammer tap.

Dealing With Overheating Breakdowns

I carry 2½ gallons of water for adding to cooling systems. I also carry a roll of duct tape which is useful for many things, including very temporary mending of coolant hoses with small leaks – just enough so the vehicle can be driven to a shop for hose replacement. Better than duct tape is special tape for temporary mending of hoses – available at most car parts stores. If the vehicle has already been turned off due to overheating, try adding coolant (water will work as a stopgap measure), turning off the AC and turning up the heater, and with the ignition turned off, tapping the motors of the electric cooling fans if they will not turn when the ignition is on.

WARNING: overheated engines usually have coolant at temperatures above water's boiling point, so there should be no attempt to add coolant until the engine has had time to cool down a bit, perhaps 20 minutes. I always use leather gloves and a towel to handle the radiator cap, in order to prevent being scalded. Never add cold water to a hot engine cooling system. This can cause the engine block to crack.

Walt Recommends: During summer months, whether or not your vehicle has had a history of overheating, carry a gallon jug of water and a funnel and a roll of hose mending tape. If the vehicle has a history of overheating, take it to a good mechanic as prevention.

Chapter 6

Engine Cuts Off and Will Not Re-start

Very often the causes for engine cut-off and failure to restart are simply: 1) loose battery cables, and/or 2) dead battery. Sometimes the problem also can be a bad alternator, or occasionally just a faulty fuel pump cutoff switch (on Ford Motor Company vehicles), blown fuel pump fuse, or loose connection of wires to spark plugs.

Loose Battery Cables

The Chevrolet Suburban was stopped on the shoulder of Interstate 10 on a very hot day; the engine was off, all windows were down. The mother and her young son were sweltering and red-faced; he was crying. She was on her cell phone anxiously telling her husband, some 100 miles away, that she thought the problem was a bad alternator and asking him where she could find one. I asked her what had happened; she replied that the engine had just died and she had recently filled up with gas; the instrument lights had blinked and "chirped" just before the engine died. I asked her to pop her hood and turn on the headlights. The headlights would not come on.

After raising the hood I first checked battery connectors for tightness; both were loose. <u>If either connector can be moved at all by hand it is too loose and likely is preventing the battery from providing juice to the vehicle's ignition system.</u> This is a very common problem. It's the second thing I check when an engine has "just cut off" (the first thing I ask is, "Do you have gas?"). Many General Motors vehicles made before 2007 have relatively small side-mounted battery connectors. I tightened the nuts for both connectors until I could no longer move the connectors by hand, and then just a little more (too much tightening of these side mounted clamps can result in a battery puncture). I asked her to start the engine; it started right away and kept running. She was ecstatic! A few days later her very nice thank you note arrived by mail.

GM vehicles with small side-mounted battery connectors use a 5/16-inch wrench (same as 8mm). For some reason these connectors tend to loosen more often than others; maybe that's why GM switched in 2007 to batteries with the larger top-mounted posts.

Walt Recommends: For GM vehicles with small side-mounted battery connectors, keep handy in your glove compartment a flat 5/16-inch, or 8mm, "combination" wrench ("open" on one end; "box" on the other), or ¼-inch drive socket wrench (with 8mm socket). About once every two months, check the connectors' tightness by trying to twist them by hand. Use the wrench to keep the battery clamps tight. Monkey wrenches, adjustable with thumb screw, have a bulky head, so they are not flat or small enough to work.

Battery Connection Cleaning

I had a similar experience with a Ford Mustang, which had top-mounted battery posts for the clamps to fasten to. Typically, top-mounted battery posts develop a powdered light green crud buildup which insulates the battery from its cables (as do side-mounted connectors). When this is the case I first clean the posts and clamps with a battery terminal brush. Then I tighten the nuts for both clamps.

Cleaning battery clamp

Cleaning battery post

The "Paperclip Trick"

In the case of this Mustang, the nuts for the battery clamps could not be tightened any more, but the clamps were still loose. So, I reached into my small stash of paperclips, and with wire cutters, clipped several segments of paperclip the same length as the battery posts (about 1 inch). After loosening the battery clamps, I slid two segments of paperclip inside each clamp alongside the posts – to provide slightly more bulk to the posts – just enough so that the clamps now could grab the posts and be tightened.

Then, with a hammer, I gently tapped on the ends of the paper-clip segments and on the top portions of the clamps so they would slide all the way down the posts to the battery. After tightening the clamps I asked him to start the engine; it started right away and kept running. Victory!

Using a small nail instead of paper clip works too.

Cutting a small piece of paper clip to insert between battery post and clamp for added bulk

The most basic thing here is to periodically check the tightness of your battery clamps; if they can be moved at all by hand you should tighten them.

NOTE: Take extra care to never allow a metal tool, such as wrench, wire cutters, or screw driver, to touch both battery terminals at the same time!

Combination wrench is the best tool to keep battery clamps tight.

Walt Recommends: Keep the correctly-sized thin, flat "combination" wrench ("open" on one end; "box" on the other) handy in your glove compartment. Adjustable monkey wrenches are not flat or small enough to be useful. The range of wrench sizes for top-mounted battery clamps is 8mm – 13mm (the most common size is 10mm). You'll have to determine the correct size (sample with a friend's wrenches, or ask at an auto parts store; they'll be glad to then sell you a wrench). Each of my cars, and each of my kids' cars, has a flat combination wrench of the correct size (all are 10mm) in its glove compartment.

If you have tried to tighten the clamps, yet they can still be moved by hand, remember the "paperclip trick", even if it is a temporary measure.

Jumper Cables

Jumper cables can save the day by jump-starting an engine with dead battery and charging another vehicle's dead battery.

Correct Sequence When Using Jumper Cables to Jump Start another Vehicle With Dead or Weak Battery:

1. Ensure that the vehicles are not touching, and the "booster" vehicle's engine is not running.

2. Ensure that no cable ends are touching each other or dangling in either engine compartment where they could be snagged by a running engine.

3. Connect one of the "positive" cable ends (usually with a red clamp) to the positive terminal of the dead/weak battery (marked with a "+" on the battery).

4. Connect the other end of the "positive" cable (with red clamp) to the positive terminal of the booster battery (confirm that a "+" is next to the battery terminal).

5. Connect the "negative" cable end (usually with a black clamp) to the negative battery terminal of the booster vehicle (marked with a "-"on the battery).

6. Connect the other end of the "negative" cable to an unpainted metal surface on the engine of the vehicle with the dead/weak battery.

7. Start the booster vehicle's engine.

8. Let the booster vehicle's engine run for a few minutes to allow the dead battery to receive some initial charge.

9. Start the engine of the vehicle with dead/weak battery.

10. Remove cables in reverse sequence.

NOTE: If the engine of the vehicle with dead/weak battery stops running when jumper cables are removed, this indicates that the dead/weak vehicle's alternator is not working. In this case, the booster vehicle probably can be used to charge the boosted vehicle's battery sufficiently for a short drive. See the "Dead Battery/Bad Alternator" section in this chapter.

Some larger diesel engines in pickups use two 12-volt batteries connected in parallel, providing total output of 12 volts but with additional cranking capacity. Such dual-battery diesels can function in either a "booster" or "boosted" role with another dual-battery vehicle or with a single-battery vehicle, and vice versa. With dual-battery vehicles, one of the batteries, normally on the passenger side of the engine compartment, will have thicker cables than the other. Use the battery with thicker cables during jump starts.

These larger diesel engines require a healthy battery for the glow plugs, electric fuel pump, and starter. If the glow plugs don't get replaced after a couple hundred thousand miles, then cold starting can be a true chore. The battery must be able to provide electrical power to spin the fuel pressure up to minimum or it will never start, and stopping for lunch is enough time for the engine to cool so that a weak battery will not start it.

Car batteries are two general types: "Maintenance free" and "Non-maintenance free". Maintenance free batteries are sealed. Unless water covers the rib-like cells inside the non-maintenance free battery, the battery likely will not accept or retain any charge.

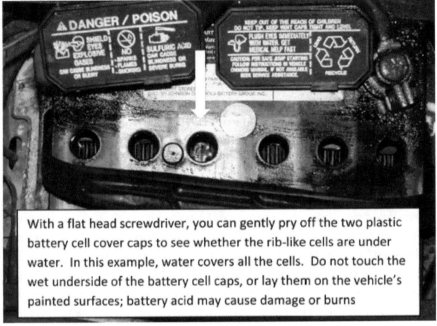

With a flat head screwdriver, you can gently pry off the two plastic battery cell cover caps to see whether the rib-like cells are under water. In this example, water covers all the cells. Do not touch the wet underside of the battery cell caps, or lay them on the vehicle's painted surfaces; battery acid may cause damage or burns

Adding water (ideally distilled, but tap water will work in a pinch) can enable a dry battery to function, perhaps degraded and temporarily.

Dead Battery/Bad Alternator Charging Problems

The Mitsubishi Eclipse sports car was broken down on the shoulder of Interstate 10 at mid-afternoon. The driver, a 30-something year old man, told me he had recently filled up with gas, and that his engine just stopped running. I checked his battery clamps; they were tight. I asked him to turn on his headlights; they would not come on – which was a good indicator that his battery was dead. I checked the water inside the battery to see whether the battery was likely to accept and hold a charge; water covered the tops of the cells inside the battery, a good indicator (but not proof, without using a battery tester) that the battery was OK.

Bad Alternator – Not Always a Show Stopper if Battery Will Accept a Charge

I connected my 20-foot jumper cables from my battery to the Mitsubishi Eclipse battery (plus to plus; minus to negative ground), which enabled him to start the engine, but his engine stopped as soon as I disconnected the cables. This meant that his alternator likely was not working and was failing to charge his battery. If his battery was OK, it should be able to accept a charge from a working alternator and, in turn, provide juice necessary for the ignition system to work and keep the engine running – for a while.

I left the jumper cables on from my battery to his battery and ground, <u>with my engine running so that my alternator was charging his battery</u>. I had him turn off all his electricity-consuming devices, including his engine, because they would drain current from his battery and slow the process of charging his battery.

Twenty minutes of this charged his battery enough so that even without a working alternator, his battery was able to provide enough juice to the ignition system to drive some 40 miles to a repair shop. He started his engine just before I disconnected the jumper cables, and he drove to the shop. I followed him. Amazing!

Since then I have used this procedure some 25 times.

I had to use this technique to make it home at night (my alternator had gone bad). My son's pickup charged my car's battery, but since I had to use my headlights, I could get only 7-8 miles per charge. He followed me home and had to repeat the charging process twice. Lesson here: since headlights consume so much juice, plan on a much shorter driving range using this technique at night.

Normally before your battery goes dead and/or your alternator fails, the warning will be dimming instrument lights and/or a weak engine start. When the "battery" light on the dashboard comes on while driving, it usually means that the battery is no longer being charged by the alternator. Your vehicle is telling you it needs immediate attention. Do not put off getting your electrical system checked, or you'll end up getting stranded. Cold weather can rob batteries of ability to turn over an engine, especially one with cold-thickened motor oil. This makes jumper cables especially useful during cold weather.

Thin Jumper Cables vs. Thick jumper Cables.

At a Walmart near Fayetteville, NC, I spotted a 1995 Toyota Camry with hood up, so I parked next to it. A middle age guy was trying to install a belt for his alternator. When I arrived I offered use of my tools, but he declined any assistance. Thirty minutes later when I returned to my car he was still there, having just finished his task. He told me the car was his daughter's and she had run down the battery since the alternator belt had broken, and he likely would need a jump. We tried unsuccessfully with my portable jumper battery (not powerful enough), so I returned to my trunk for my heavy duty 2-gauge cables. Just then a fellow in a Ford Explorer pulled into a parking space front-to-front with the Camry, saw what was going on, and tried with his skinny jumper cables to jump the Camry. No go. Then we hooked up my cables from the Explorer to the Camry and the car started right up. Lesson here is that there's no substitute for a heavy duty set of jumper cables. Smiles and handshakes, and we split.

Walt Recommends:

1. Get 20-foot jumper cables with at least 4-gauge copper wiring (2-gauge is better), which permits jumps with vehicles in single file on the shoulder of a highway, and precludes having to put vehicles front-to-front, or even side-by-side. Keep the cables in your vehicle. Recently I replaced my old portable jumper battery since it was getting weak. Its replacement is a very highly

rated small portable jumper battery, "Jump n Carry model JNC660". This battery has plenty of power (1,700 peak amps) to start a large V-8 engine with dead battery. Now I no longer need to use jumper cables so often for jump starts, but I still use them to charge other batteries.

2. Do not use electrically-powered items, such as the vehicle sound system, while the engine is off (and not recharging the battery) since this is likely to weaken the battery so that it will not permit starting the engine. This has happened several times with folks I have assisted for a flat tire when the driver and I took the flat to a tire store. Family members waited for our return in the broken down vehicle, listening to music.

20-feet long jumper cables provide best flexibility. Use thick 2-gauge for best results.

Push Start

The "push start" technique of jump starting an engine with dead battery works only with vehicles with manual transmission and a working alternator. Push starting could be used to start a vehicle disabled along a highway, say, where a loose battery clamp has been tightened but the battery is dead. At least two people are required: one sits in the driver seat while others push the vehicle from behind, manually or with another vehicle. The need for a pusher diminishes if the vehicle with dead battery is on a downhill slope and can roll forward freely and gain speed. The driver turns the ignition switch to "on" or the "running" position, depresses the clutch pedal, and puts the transmission lever in second gear. When the vehicle's forward rolling

speed reaches 5 mph the driver lets out the clutch quickly and simultaneously presses slightly on the accelerator to start the engine. The driver must
immediately then depress the clutch pedal to remove load from the engine
so it can continue to run. NOTE: The driver should never multi-task as a
pusher; drivers attempting to do so have been inadvertently run over by their
own vehicles.

Fuel Pump Cutoff Switches in Ford Motor Company Vehicles

As far as I know (and I have checked recently with service managers at Ford
dealerships) all Ford Motor Company vehicles (Ford, Mercury, Lincoln) use
an inertia switch to deactivate the fuel pump in a collision in order to prevent
a fire. This is an excellent safety feature.

On two or three occasions, I have encountered broken down Fords whose
drivers told me that their engines had "just shut off"; the problem was an
inertia fuel pump cutoff switch which had tripped for some reason other
than a collision. The vehicle owner's manual is usually the best guide for
locating the switch. My experience is that in pickups and vans, the switch
is inside the cab, behind a flap in the lower right side panel near the front
passenger's right knee. In sedans, the switch has been either in the trunk in
the left side panel, or inside the car near the right front passenger's right foot.
It's common for an inertia switch to disengage during severe off-road driving
or a minor collision. Simply pushing down the red button located at the top
of the inertia switch will reset the switch. So now when I encounter a Ford
Motor Company vehicle whose engine has "just cut off", I include a check of
the fuel pump cutoff switch in my diagnosis.

Chapter Summary:

1. Loose and/or dirty battery connections often cause "engine cut-off"; best
   remedy is to check connectors and keep them tight and clean.

2. Jumper cables 20-feet long are by far the best tool to jump start an engine, or charge a dead battery caused by bad alternator.

3. Skinny jumper cables do not work nearly as well as ones with thicker cable (at least 4-gauge; 2-gauge is better).

4. If your vehicle is a Ford Motor Company product, locate its fuel pump cut-off switch.

Chapter 7

Motorist is Locked out of Vehicle

Have you ever locked yourself out of your vehicle? This happens only occasionally, typically when changing your routine for exiting the vehicle and mistakenly leaving your keys inside when the doors are locked or when for some reason the regular key has been lost or stolen (which can be aggravated if the car battery is dead). Being locked out has happened to me a few times and to all of my kids.

In 2011, I encountered a pickup truck with a horse trailer in tow on the shoulder of Interstate 95. The couple with the pickup had just changed a flat tire on the trailer, but now they were locked out of their pickup. Evidently, the husband, after inadvertently locking the pickup's doors, had left the vehicle's keys on the driver seat, and a gust from a passing 18-wheeler blew the driver door shut. The couple had been there for 30 minutes trying unsuccessfully to unlock a door. Luckily I had some "special tools" (wedges to pry a small gap between a vehicle door and body, inflatable devices to enlarge the gap, and specially shaped steel rods which pass through the gap and engage an unlock mechanism) and was able to unlock their door.

In another case, my son's mother-in-law was locked out of her Honda Odyssey at my son's house. She had left the vehicle's keys on the driver seat and had closed the unlocked door. She had not seen my son's cat jump into her vehicle, and before long the cat stepped on the lock switch on the armrest, locking all doors. Responding to her call for assistance I went over and unlocked the door with my "special tools".

Recently, at a gas station in Fayetteville, the driver of the car on the other side of my pump cursed that he had just locked his keys in his car. Again, "special tools" to the rescue.

I'm not going to discuss here the art of unlocking car doors. Instead, the question is, "How to best prevent getting locked out in the first place?"

Dealing with Lock Outs

The best solution to prevent being locked out of one's vehicle is to keep a spare key for only the driver's door in a magnetic keybox under the vehicle. All my vehicles and now all my kids' vehicles (and my son's mother-in-law's Odyssey) have spare keys in keyboxes attached to the vehicles' undercarriages with strong magnets. These keys, without expensive transponders and available for around $10 from a new car dealer, locksmith, or in some cases your local hardware store, will unlock the driver's door mechanically, but will not (except for older vehicles using keys without transponders) activate the vehicle's ignition. Inside the vehicles I have hidden spare keys (spare ignition key or valet key) with transponders which can activate the vehicle's ignition. I do not advocate storing expensive keys with transponders under a vehicle since the keys could get wet and suffer damage to their electronics; theoretically, they also could be lost, but that has never happened to me in 25 years. These magnetic keyboxes are sold at Lowes and other hardware stores for less than $2. I cannot think of a better bargain.

If you return from vacation and find your vehicle at the airport parking lot with no key and a dead battery from the dome light's being left on, a fob entry system will not unlock your door, but an unlocked door is necessary in order to pop the hood for a jump start. At least a door key from the keybox will permit getting into your vehicle and setting up a jump start.

Walt Recommends: Use a magnetic keybox (be sure to get one with two magnets) to store a spare <u>door key</u> under the vehicle. For newer cars with high tech ignition keys, you can get a $10 "dumb" key without transponder, which will work only on the driver's door. Stash a key with transponder for the ignition inside the vehicle (a valet key works here). Important: the box needs to be positioned on a flat, vertical surface with no thick corrosion insulation, which could weaken the magnets' grip. Using vertical surfaces will prevent the box from being scraped off should the vehicle bottom out.

NOTE: A friend, who owns a late model Lexus with keyless feature whose ignition keys emit Radio Frequency (RF) signals, told me that stashing an ignition key in his car would not work since the car would not lock if an ignition key were inside. I checked with a Lexus "technology specialist" who told me his solution: Wrap the ignition key in aluminum foil, which would act as a shield to the key's RF emissions. This is a great example of a low-tech solution!

Magnetic keybox on flat, smooth, <u>vertical</u> steel surface without sprayed-on corrosion-resistant insulation provides best grip and protection from being scraped off if vehicle bottoms out.

Occasionally, a skeptic of hiding an extra key in a magnetic keybox under the car's frame has told me that it makes vehicle theft easier. Well, I have never read or heard about a thief's finding a key under a car. There are several places under a vehicle where the magnetic keybox could be hidden – making it highly unlikely to be found; besides, most thieves are too lazy and rushed to get down on the ground and search for a box which may or may not even be there. Thieves almost always steal vehicles requiring least effort: unoccupied with engine running, ignition keys left in the ignition or in plain view and/ or with a screw driver in older vehicles without transponders in ignition keys. Also, the key for newer vehicles I suggest stashing under the car is without transponder so it would only unlock the driver's door and not activate the ignition.

Chapter Summary:

1. Being locked out of your car can happen to you.

2. Plan ahead by hiding a spare door key in a magnetic keybox under your car.

3. Stash inside your vehicle a spare key with transponder for the ignition, if applicable.

Chapter 8

Suggested Items to Contend with Vehicle Breakdowns

The more items on the "suggested" list below that you have <u>in your vehicle</u> (not left behind in your garage) the better your chances are of making your own good luck if your vehicle breaks down. "Better to have it and not need it, than to need it and not have it." Most of these items are small and light in weight, easily permitting storage in a car trunk; some items should have come with your vehicle and already be stowed with it. Items are listed in the priority sequence I would recommend (most important first):

- Complete set of tire-changing tools, <u>designed for your vehicle</u>. Includes: lug wrench, jack (with all components), <u>key to the locking lug nuts</u> and <u>key to gain access to the spare tire</u> (not a common item, but you need to check – easy: try to remove the spare without a key). These items should already be in your vehicle, but you need to confirm it. Trust but verify.

- Serviceable, fully inflated spare tire, <u>made for your vehicle</u>. Should already be in your vehicle, but you need to confirm it (and check the tire's air pressure and age: six years or less). Trust but verify.

- Cell phone, with battery charger, to summon help, if needed. This item likely would not be kept in the vehicle, but carried by the driver.

- Magnetic keybox (containing a car door key) to prevent being locked out of your vehicle. This would be secured under the vehicle, not in an inside-the-vehicle storage place.

Layout of all items listed below.

"Suggested" Items Not Already Stowed with Vehicle or Normally Carried by the Driver

NOTE: Several items in the layout above and listed below are associated with ½-inch drive sockets to loosen, remove and replace lug nuts; however, none of these pieces should be needed if the vehicle's rims are "stock" and not aftermarket – which likely means that the lug nuts can be managed using either the vehicle's stock lug wrench or a 4-way lug wrench. Here again, "trust but verify" that a lug wrench will work with your vehicle's rims and lug nuts. If not, then go with sockets. Are these items available already, pre-packaged and sold in stores or on line? I doubt it; such kits typically consist of marginally useful variants: skinny, short jumper cables; 4-way lug wrenches too small to permit "breaking" really tight lug nuts; and kits do not include most of the other items at all.

- Road atlas, to help determine your location if you are far from home, your GPS is not working, and you need to call for help. My atlas lists all Walmart stores, an excellent source for good deals on tires nationwide – essential if motorist's GPS does not work or is unable to locate other major tire dealers, such as Pep Boys (which typically stays open later than most: Monday thru Saturday until 9 PM; Sundays until 6 PM).

- Old beach towel to pad your knees while kneeling, and to spread out to lie on to keep from getting dirty while on the ground to position a vehicle jack or to remove or mount tires.

- Cheap tarp for use with, or in lieu of, beach towel when ground is wet.

- Tire pressure gauge calibrated to at least 60 psi (pressure required for most donut spare tires to be useful and safe). Tires for some heavy pick-ups, vans, trailers and campers require even higher tire pressure, so the gauge then would need to register greater than 60 psi.

- 12-volt air compressor, to inflate tires to correct operating pressures. Get 12-volt power from a car cigarette lighter or portable jumper battery.

- Cheater bar (1" X 2 feet long steel pipe: $8 at hardware stores) to slip over the handle of your vehicle lug wrench or breaker bar for extra leverage in case lug nuts are on too tightly. Also can be used as a lever to lift a heavy spare tire that final ¼-inch, while mounting it on the vehicle's wheel, to facilitate mating wheel lugs with holes in the rim.

- 4-way lug wrench (get a large one, at least 22") for good leverage and to quickly "spin off/on" lug nuts, especially if vehicle has no lug wrench.

Walt Recommends: Ken-Tool model "35657", a heavy-duty 23-inch model.

- Pair of heavy leather work gloves to protect hands from exposed steel wires from blown out tires.

- Set of 3 reflecting warning triangles.

- Light-reflecting vest (bright orange or yellow, with white reflecting strips).

- Pliers (or vise-grips), to gain sufficient leverage to loosen corroded wing nuts securing spare tires to vehicles (in car trunks and mini-vans and small SUVs).

- Piece of treated plywood board 8" X 8"X ½" thick to place under vehicle jack to distribute the vehicle's weight on soft/uneven ground, sand, and ground vegetation to stabilize the jack and prevent it from sinking or sliding.

- Headlamp (fits on a strap around your head: works much better than a flashlight) in case the breakdown occurs at night. Check its batteries.

- Battery terminal brush – includes male and female components to clean both posts and clamps.

- Jumper cables: Thick, heavy duty (2- or 4-gauge), 20-feet long cables to permit jump starts, and remote battery charges, without having to position vehicles front-to-front, or even side-by-side.

- Portable jumper battery with short cables can be used to jump start an engine with a weak battery and power a 12-volt air compressor or cell phone. Typically, portable jumper batteries feature a lamp to illuminate night time tire changes, and jumps. These batteries require charging after each use, and monthly. Total loss of charge kills these batteries.

- Flat, thin "combination" wrench ("open" on one end; "box" on the other), or ¼-inch drive socket wrench, for battery clamps: Range of sizes of nuts on battery clamps is 8mm - 13mm. Most common size is 10mm. Adjustable monkey wrenches do not work since their heads are too thick and bulky.

- 1-gallon gas can (empty) which can be used to bring fuel from a gas station.

- Roll of duct tape, or hose repair tape, for temporary repairs to a vehicle hose leaking coolant, or to secure loose trim as result of a minor accident.

- Breaker bar (18-24 inches long, ½-inch drive) for use with ½-inch drive extension bar and sockets, to "break" (loosen) lug nuts, <u>especially when the gap around "aftermarket" rims' lug nut holes is too small to allow lug wrench fit.</u> It's good to have a ½-inch drive ratchet wrench, or old-fashioned "speed wrench" to expedite turning and removing the nuts once they are "broken" (and to expedite replacing the nuts during mounting of the spare tire rim so that the nuts are snug). Breaker bar then is useful when tightening the lug nuts.

- Socket (½-inch drive) to fit lug nuts, for use with breaker bar, ratchet wrench, extension bar, and speed wrench. Deep socket adds flexibility when lugs protrude significantly beyond lug nuts (occurs often on heavy duty vans and pickups).

- Extension bar (best length depends on your rim configuration) for ½-inch drive with socket; critical when must access nuts in a deep dish rim. Extension bars can be joined end-to-end for increased standoff.

- Set of two tough plastic chocks to place under the wheel diagonally opposite the wheel with flat tire, to prevent the vehicle from rolling while being lifted and while jacked up.

- Can of "PB Penetrating Catalyst", or "Liquid Wrench" to spray on stubborn/rusted nuts to facilitate removal. This stuff works like magic.

- Gallon of water, in case the engine cooling system has run low, and for long trips – especially in hot weather or in mountains if your vehicle's engine has shown any inclination to overheat. Be extremely careful when adding fluid to a hot cooling system, to prevent being scalded. Use an old towel and heavy gloves while removing the cap to the cooling system (wait a while, say 20 minutes, for the heat to dissipate). Adding water should be only a temporary measure when 50/50 water/antifreeze mix is unavailable, until a mechanic can check the cooling system. Your water also can be used to refill cells of non-maintenance free vehicle batteries, which need this fluid in order to acquire and retain a charge.

- Extra quart of engine oil, in case the engine overheats and turns out to be low on oil.

- Funnels to prevent waste and spills when pouring fuel, oil, water or coolant.

Stowage of Items on "Suggested" List

Almost all items on my "Suggested" list above (and in the layout shown in the previous photo) will fit in a shallow 34-quart plastic tub, which fits with much room to spare in the small trunk of my 1989 Honda Accord. Only the warning triangles, beach towel, lightweight tarp, and small tool bag are not in the tub. The smaller items fit in the black bag. Some of these items may seem a bit too bulky for your vehicle's storage capacity (perhaps the water jug, empty gas can, speed wrench); if so, you should work from the bottom of the prioritized list when deleting items.

Additional Items Walt Carries "On Patrol" (Which are NOT Suggested for, or Needed by, the Average Driver)....

Everything on my "Suggested" list above, and much, much more, fits nicely in the trunk of my Honda Accord. Useful items in my trunk <u>besides items on the "suggested" list</u> (since the everyday driver doesn't need them) include: Low-profile rolling hydraulic jack (for fast lifts on most vehicles); 12-ton bottle jack for lifting heavy vehicles with lots of ground clearance; jack for a heavy duty Chevrolet pickup, raised and lowered by turning a long shaft, which permits lifts of pickups and vans where lift points are far from the side of the vehicle (I do not get under any vehicle while jacking it up); low-profile scissors jack in case there is no room to use my hydraulic jack; two pieces of 12"X30"X2" lumber to go under jacks (especially the rolling hydraulic jack) for stability and additional elevation, if required; two strips of 22-gauge steel 8"X30" to place under my rolling hydraulic jack to provide a smooth rolling surface when limited ground clearance precludes use of my lumber; 25 treated plywood squares, 8"X8"X½, to improvise ramps for trailer tire changes and shore up my other lumber to ensure that my lifts are vertical and safe; jack stand to prop a vehicle up while relocating lift points in difficult jobs; tire plug kit; small plastic spray bottle of soapy water to apply to a tire's surfaces to identify possible leaks during inflation when progress seems slow; a 2-gallon metal can full of gasoline; "special tools" door unlock kit; another 1½-gallons of water; 4 additional quarts of oil; quart of automatic transmission fluid; several funnels; crowbar; bolt cutters; steel mallet; tool bag with large collection of wrenches, pliers, screw drivers, extension bars, wire cutters and sockets (some to defeat rounded lug nuts, and wheel locks when motorist cannot find his wheel lock key); hacksaw; heavy-duty folding knife/box cutter for cutting plastic and rubber pieces from a damaged vehicle which scrape the ground or interfere with the vehicle's wheel movement; can of ether-based engine starter primer; tow strap; two "9-in-1 Safety Puck" red flashing LEDs; fire extinguisher; old bedsheet and large plastic bag for protecting the inside of my car from a dirty/wet flat tire on rim when carrying it to a tire store (with stranded motorist) for repair/replacement when he has no spare; and several bottles of drinking water. Use of this photo is with permission of executive editor of "Fayetteville Observer" newspaper.

Chapter 9

Win-Win Hobby

In our crazy world of terrorism, poverty, crime and scandals each of us would be better off if he had a hobby which provided 1) escape from the negative, 2) immersion in the positive, 3) wholesome, cheap entertainment, and 4) satisfaction from helping someone in a jam. I have found such a hobby: stopping for and assisting motorists in broken down vehicles. I call it my "Win-Win Hobby"; everyone involved wins: I win because the deed makes me feel good, and the motorist wins because he is no longer immobilized and stranded under conditions which could endanger his safety and health.

Now, this book's readers will also win, since they will be empowered to bail themselves out of the most common situations which strand motorists. Expecting readers to take this stuff as far as I have would be a stretch, but I thought I'd provide a taste of my motives anyway – just in case.

Adopting this hobby has given me a new outlook on driving – even on living. Before, driving always meant getting from point A to B as quickly and safely as possible by careful lane selection and watching all other vehicles to see who would likely create opportunities to advance in traffic. Occasionally, when I am not alone in my car or I must be somewhere and there is no time to stop for others, I still drive that way; after all, this is a hobby, not a job.

But now most often my focus is to stay in the right lane, drive at the speed limit, and look for vehicles broken down or with conditions predicting trouble (such as a low tire). This mindset of always looking for someone to help, and knowing that I can and will help, is wonderfully and extremely empowering, liberating and exciting. My thought is, "I've got a really cool capability, and I can't wait to show up where someone is in a jam and really make his day". Then after the problem is solved and they are so grateful, I normally ask them to do the same for someone else. For me, the rush begins when I first see the flashing lights (on a highway) or a hood up (in a parking lot), and it lasts for hours after the assist is done.

Sometimes the motorist will insist on paying money, but I always decline since accepting payment could indicate that my real motive was monetary gain. If he strongly insists on paying, I'll accept it since I assume this means that he needed to provide that kind of thanks.

The thrill during and just after helping someone is addicting. The more difficult and successful the effort, the more relief I can bring, and the more assists during a trip, the more addicting it becomes. So much so that besides stopping for others during normal trips I regularly go to Interstate 95 which passes by my town of Eastover, North Carolina, and "patrol" for broken down vehicles. When I lived in Katy, Texas (near Houston), Interstate 10 was my turf.

A deputy sheriff helps secure the scene on a hot day during one of my assists along Interstate 10 in Texas. The lady was pregnant with two small children in the vehicle. Her right rear tire has blown out and shredded. I am under the Chevy Suburban trying to adjust the long plastic tube that aligns the vehicle's tire changing tool with the mechanism to lower her spare tire (I had never before encountered this problem, so I was learning this fix by on-the-job training). Normally, I don't have a photographer with me, but this time a reporter/photographer from a local magazine wanted to get a shot of me "in action" for an article. I could not have set this up better if I had tried: We encountered this Suburban a mere 10 minutes into our "patrol". My trusty 1989 white Honda Accord coupe with trunk full of tools is in front of the Suburban. That old car now has 525,000 miles on it, testimony to regular maintenance (and great design). It has broken down four times; once with a flat tire (which I changed myself), once with a broken hose (which I could not reach to fix), once with a broken distributor rotor (very luckily, in front of a Honda dealer, where I pushed it in myself for repair); and once with a bad alternator and dead battery (see Chapter 6 section, "Bad Alternator"). Use of this photo is with permission of the executive publisher of "Absolutely Katy" magazine.

Safety during stops is top priority; I have included a chapter on it in this book; other chapters abound with safety tips. Traveling in the right lane at the speed limit (while most others are exceeding it) means that the speeders normally have already begun to pass, so they are in another lane. This tends to prevent their dangerous tailgating of me, leaving sufficient room for others behind me to also change lanes once I see a breakdown, let up on the gas, put on my right turn signal and start tapping my brakes. If I can pull over safely on the shoulder I will; otherwise, I'll continue to the first exit, circle back and try again. I always pull in front of the disabled vehicle so that I have plenty of room to slow down and stop, and the occupants of that vehicle can see me clearly so as not to be surprised and alarmed. I always pull over far enough to exit my vehicle safely. If there is no shoulder or other safe place to pull over, I don't stop at all.

Stops during daylight are much safer than at night. I am much less inclined to stop at all at night without a "drive by" first to see who is in the vehicle and assess the situation. A family with children is a much safer bet than all young male adults. Likewise, a well-lit area is much safer than one without any lighting.

While pulling over (day or night), after stopping, and while backing up to the disabled vehicle I look carefully for signs of possible hostility or unusual behavior. The same applies as I exit my vehicle and approach the other. Only once have I decided to call off the assist before talking to anyone; during a daylight stop for a Ford pickup on Interstate 10 near Houston I spotted an open bottle of whiskey on the console beside the driver, and there was some appearance of a physical assault in progress in the back seat of the vehicle. I immediately returned to my car and departed. Then, using my cell phone, I reported the situation to the police.

My primary safety concern once stopped is being hit by an oncoming vehicle. So my first actions, especially during darkness, poor visibility, or when the traffic is heavy, are to don my reflecting vest, have the assisted vehicle's driver turn on his hazard warning flashers, and put out three reflective warning triangles which stay out until the assist is done. Recently I acquired two "9-in-1 Safety Puck" red flashing LEDs which go, with their magnet mounts, on the rear of the disabled vehicle at night.

My goal is to complete the assist as quickly as possible to minimize exposure to oncoming vehicles. This means knowing how to handle a variety of reasons for breakdown and having the proper equipment: several jacks, sockets, 12-volt air compressor, jumper cables, and other tools for a wide variety of situations.

Roadside assisting is truly "win-win": fun, entertaining, positive, useful, extremely rewarding, and inexpensive. It's not for everyone, and I do not advocate it if you are not otherwise inclined to help others while being mindful of some inherent risk. But there are plenty of appreciative folks whose vehicles break down, for all of us who want to do it and make a difference. You can help even if you don't care to be as fully equipped as I am, with just a few extra items in your trunk.

Walt's Top 10 Reasons for Making Roadside Assists

1. Enhances self-respect for "doing the right thing" habitually; also encourages respect from others.

2. Sets a good example for one's children, grandchildren, and associates – not to mention those assisted. At the end of most assists I eyeball the assisted motorist and tell him (typically as he tries to pay me), "Do this for someone else; pay it forward. That's my message." They all say they will.

3. Improves one's capability to help not only others with disabled vehicles, but one's self too: I used the technique of charging another vehicle's battery to rescue myself one night when my alternator died. My son's vehicle provided the alternator to charge my dead battery; three separate charges were needed to get home since I had to use headlights.

4. "Gives back" to a society which has been so good to me and my family. Keeps me sharp so I can provide highly useful, relevant advice to the driver education community as they develop standardized curricula for teachers and students; also so I can pass on instructive tips to the public via media interviews.

5. Improves race relations: Due largely to local demographics 50% of those I assisted in Texas were non-whites; 60% of those I assist around Fayetteville, NC, are blacks. With the very few who initially have an "attitude", everything changes once they realize I'm really there, willing, and able, to help them. Just think of the potential for that in today's polarized society. In light of disharmony between police and some minority groups I am encouraging law enforcement to reach out by performing simple roadside assists (primarily tire changes, due to police concerns about liability) when operational priorities permit. My proposal uses this book as a foundation, expanded by a supplementary list of tips and equipment and a training video – all for export for use as in-house training for law enforcement. Link to the free training video is on my website: http://www.roadsidesurvival.com/

6. Meet interesting people: bank presidents, sheriff deputies, personal trainers, real estate executives, doctors, lawyers, teachers, college students, veterans, and regular folks of all ages, races and colors. Normally I cannot tell before an assist whether the folks I will meet are white, black, purple, beautiful or ugly. I still exchange emails with several for whom I have stopped.

7. Driving anywhere, any time (except to an appointment) is a totally different experience when one's primary agenda is spotting, stopping for, and assisting someone in a disabled vehicle. The anticipation, when rounding a curve or cresting a hill, is exciting (helps keep me awake on long trips), empowering and therapeutic, yet stress-relieving.

8. Provides relatively inexpensive entertainment and even some exercise: compare the cost of gas for a 55-mile "patrol" on the interstate ($4) to the cost of a round of golf, or going to a movie.

9. Provides the excitement and challenge of solving different problems with each assist; I often learn something new, both on site from experience and afterward from research.

10. Focusing on others' well-being, as well as how to conduct safe assists, instills a frame of mind which enhances one's own safety and security while driving.

Glossary of Terms

Aftermarket: A term describing any component or tool of a vehicle which did not come with that vehicle when it was new. Most often, this term refers to vehicle rims and tires which have replaced the originals; but it could also refer to a tool such as a different jack or lug wrench used in lieu of the vehicle's original equipment.

Breaker Bar: Steel rod, 18-20 inches long, with smooth handle at one end and an articulating ½-inch drive male fitting at the other end. Provides excellent leverage when using ½-inch drive sockets and extension bar to loosen and tighten lug nuts. Useful if a lug wrench (vehicle-issued, or 4-way) will not work, either due to insufficient leverage or if the head of the lug wrench will not fit on the lug nuts (typically when the rim is aftermarket).

Cheater Bar: Piece of steel pipe, 1-inch in diameter and at least 2-feet long, to be slipped over the handle portion of a standard L-shaped lug wrench (or a breaker bar), to extend the effective handle length and provide considerably more leverage, primarily to loosen tight lug nuts, and to tighten them if the user is not strong. A cheater bar also can be used while mounting a spare tire rim, as a lever on the ground under a heavy upright spare tire, to lift the rim the last ¼-inch to align its holes with the wheel lugs so the rim will mate with the wheel lugs.

Lug Nut: Six-sided metal nut which screws on to a wheel lug to secure a rim tightly to the vehicle's wheel. Common exterior sizes of the heads of lug nuts: 17mm, 19mm, and 21mm. Larger vehicles generally use the larger lug nuts. Many German-made autos use 17mm bolts, in lieu of wheel lugs and lug nuts.

Lug Wrench: Tool which provides leverage to "break" (loosen), remove, replace, and tighten lug nuts, or bolts, which secure a rim with tire to a vehicle's wheel. Vehicles sold with spare tires come with a lug wrench, which normally consists of a heavy L-shaped steel rod with head on one end to fit over the vehicle's lug nuts, and the other, longer segment as a handle. An optional type of lug wrench, a "4-way", is shaped like a very large "plus" sign with different sized heads on each of the four ends. This wrench permits increased leverage to loosen and tighten lug nuts (using "push" and "pull" concurrently), and can be used to quickly "spin" loose lug nuts on or off a wheel. "4-way" wrenches come in many sizes (heads, and lengths of the cross-members); minimum length of cross-members for excellent leverage is 22-23 inches. Smaller "4-way" wrenches often do not provide sufficient leverage to loosen tight lug nuts.

Rim: The part of the vehicle which is secured to (and removable from) the vehicle wheel and is in contact with and supports the tire. A rim often is referred to as a "wheel", but the actual vehicle wheel is the round disc that you see once you've removed the rim from the vehicle. The vehicle's wheels contain the lugs which mate with corresponding holes in the rims. Rims are designed for specific vehicles; trying to use rims on other vehicles' wheels is rarely successful.

Spacer: A metal disk which fits between some aftermarket rims and the vehicle's wheels, in order to allow these rims to fit onto the vehicle's wheels and turn freely without rubbing against the vehicle's brakes and other vehicle parts. The only time this becomes a concern is if an original vehicle rim is used as a spare; then, the spacer must be removed from the vehicle wheel in order for the original rim to fit on the vehicle wheel. If the spacer is not removed, the wheel lugs (or likely bolts if the car is German-made) will not be long enough to secure the original rim to the vehicle.

Wheel Lugs: Parts of a vehicle's wheel (normally four or five per wheel, except for heavy duty pickups and vans which have six or more) which extend outward and fit through holes in the removable rim – on which the tire is mounted. Lug nuts screw on to the wheel lugs to ensure that the rim is fastened tightly and safely to the vehicle's wheel. NOTE: Instead of wheel lugs and lug nuts, some automobiles, mostly German-made, use heavy bolts (normally five per wheel) to fasten rims to vehicle wheels.

About the Author

Walt Brinker grew up with four sisters in a military family, living in Arkansas, Germany, Iowa, Massachusetts, New York, Kansas, France, Pennsylvania, Oklahoma, and Virginia.

He graduated from the United States Military Academy at West Point, New York, in 1966 with a Bachelor of Science degree in engineering, and was commissioned in the U.S. Army as a second lieutenant of infantry. His Army career included two combat tours in Vietnam, tactics instructor at the US Army Infantry School, troop duty in Germany and the US, Command and General Staff College, and a tour at the Pentagon on the Army Staff, working to field the Bradley Fighting Vehicle and modernize the Army's infantry battalions.

He retired from the Army as a Lieutenant Colonel in 1990. Military awards include Silver Star, two Bronze Stars for valor, two Bronze Stars for service, Purple Heart, Combat Infantryman Badge, Ranger Tab, Airborne wings, Army Staff Identification Badge, and two awards of the Legion of Merit.

In 1971, Walt married Betsy, now an accomplished designer and fabricator of costumes for mascots of professional sports teams. He and Betsy have five children and seven grandchildren. One son is a software code developer in Boston. Three other sons serve, or have served, in the U.S. Army on active duty with Infantry and Special Forces units; one of them is now an Army aviator. His daughter is a certified financial planner.

After retiring from the Army, he settled in Katy, Texas, working in management positions for two security companies, and as a project controls engineer for a large engineering and construction company. In 2010 he moved to Eastover, North Carolina, to live near grandchildren, and worked as a project manager in nearby Fayetteville.

Over the years since 1980 he has been providing free-of-charge roadside assists as a hobby. His hobby has been featured on several television and radio shows, in a local magazine article, and two newspapers: The Houston Chronicle, and The Fayetteville Observer, which runs his monthly vignettes describing actual assists and how readers can avoid such situations. He wrote this short book after deciding it was time to try to empower as many others as possible to avoid vehicle breakdowns and becoming stranded. He teaches "Roadside Survival" at Fayetteville Technical Community College, and he has been a speaker at several driver education and law enforcement conferences around the country. His website is **http://www.roadsidesurvival.com/**

CPSIA information can be obtained
at www.ICGtesting.com
Printed in the USA
BVHW061216161222
654335BV00002B/66